Living Well Without A Job

249 Eco-friendly Ways to Work Less So You Can Live More

Jesse Shelton

Copyright © 2013 by Jesse Shelton

All rights reserved.

No part of this publication may be reproduced, distributed, or transmitted in any form or by any means, including photocopying, recording, or other electronic or mechanical methods, without the prior written permission of the publisher, except in the case of brief quotations embodied in critical reviews and certain other noncommercial uses permitted by copyright law. For permission requests, write to the publisher, addressed "Attention: Permissions Coordinator," at Jesseshelt@gmail.com

Ordering Information:

Quantity sales. Special discounts are available on quantity purchases by corporations, associations, and others. For details, contact the publisher at the address above.

Publisher's Cataloging-in-Publication data

Shelton, Jesse.

Living Well Without A Job:

249 Ways to Work Less So You Can Live More

Jesse Shelton.
ISBN 978-1489533241
1. House and Home/Sustainable Living.

First Edition

Support Clean Energy

100% of all author royalties are invested in alternative energy development and infrastructure.

Thank you Jessica.

Your support and affection have helped me realize how beautiful life can be. The world is a much better place because you're in it.

And to my parents, both of whom taught me what it means to truly love for the sake of love itself and to give it no bounds.

Contents

Introduction   1

1 Starting Out: Budgets   4

2 Living in the Middle:
    The philosophy of easy life   9

3 Energy: The fastest savings   19

4 Food and Drink:
    How to get both for free   39

5 Gardening: Less work   70

6 Health, Medicine, and Cleaning:
    Natural Alternatives   82

7 Clothing and Stuff:
    How to get (free) quality products   114

8 Bikes and Biodiesel:
    A how-to for alternative transportation   130

9 Better Design, Better Life:
    Build a house that supports you   138

10 Finances:
   Make your money work for you   161

11 Play, Travel, and Community:
   Free stuff; from world-wide housing to weddings   175

12 Creating Happiness:
   The most important part   192

Preface

This book is an introduction to the easy life. It details some of the most effective ways I've found to build a lifestyle that both largely runs itself, and that requires little financial input. Because the subject is so vast, I only fully explain ideas that cannot be found in a quick online search. If I tried to fully explain everything I mention, I would still be writing 10 years from now. Therefore, I see this book as both a detailed explanation of some of the most impactful (and unconventional) ways to build a work-free life, and a source to introduce you to numerous smaller tried-and-true methods.

Although this book directly concerns building an easy, work-free life, every idea is underwritten with an overarching attention to the impacts our lives have on the world around us. My experiences have led me to believe that humankind would best serve as stewards of the world, caretakers of the environment and animals who inhabit it along with us. Because of our intellect, I believe to simply exist as a mutually-beneficial part of nature is all but impossible for human society as it exists now; it's too easy and gratifying to modify our world to better suit our needs. This is what all animals do in their own ways; beavers build dams that flood woodlands, woodpeckers drill holes that eventually bring down trees, and foraging bears leave behind a path of uprooted bushes. It is a natural way of being. However, as humans, we have an increased potential to modify the environment, to bring it out of balance, and when it balances itself once again, as it does and inevitably will, we find that other animals have disappeared, soil under our asphalt ceases to be fertile, and the rivers have become too toxic to support a diversity of life. It seems we are fulfilling our potential to modify the world, and are doing so in poorly-chosen ways.

Our intellect is part of our being, it is one of the factors that makes us human. What we are left with then, the choice we must make as individuals and a society, is how to use our intellect in a way that benefits ourselves, those around us, and the rest of the world. In this search, I have come to believe environmental stewardship is our most logical option. It's our most compassionate option. Our most peaceful option. Thankfully, our intellect can also help us build new ways of living, ways that both ensure we have comfortable, easy lives, and that our fellow animals have the same. This is the purpose behind this book, and I hope that the ideas within help you on your journey toward a happy, easy, and ultimately peaceful life.

– Jesse
Tokushima, Japan 2013

Introduction

One particularly beautiful day while in college, I had an unexpected conversation. John, a new friend of mine, was practically panicking as he shuffled back and forth between career options, unable to decide which way his life should go. He was paying a pretty penny for tuition and each semester of indecision only drove him deeper into debt. It wasn't long until I realized John was so wrapped up in his future and the way it 'should' be that he was missing out on the life he had now. I had a feeling he would always be preparing for his future, and thus one day die without having really lived. But this is what society had taught him. It's what his parents, teachers, and the media had asked of him; to succeed. And he was given a very narrow definition of success: have a respectable career, make money, buy a big house, and a start a family. Live comfortably in the middle class. The problem is that John, like most of us, felt tension with the way his life had been laid out. Yes, he made his own decisions, but they were decisions safely within the boundaries of what a 'successful' person does. Unfortunately, these choices usually don't lead to happiness.

So what was he really after? A good job, money, and a stable family were the first things out of his mouth. But as our conversation continued, it eventually ended up where most do I suppose. He simply wanted to be happy. That was it. Not money, a fancy car, or a big house. Just happiness. I've found that happiness actually has nothing to do with these things.

In today's world we have *a lot* of choices. Yet at the same time, we are only aware of these options if we have already encountered them in some way. This is the reason for this book; even though John was well-educated and had numerous mentors, he was limited to the lifestyles he had seen, but none of them matched his idea of the good life. What John wanted but couldn't quite figure out was how to build a lifestyle that is both comfortable and secure while allowing him enough free time to enjoy it. All the careers he had in mind require long hours; what he needed was to find a way to work less so he could travel for months at a time, relax in his back yard, and take off to the mountains whenever he wanted. He needed freedom. This book is designed to help him and others like him. By following the suggestions here, you can say goodbye to your 40 hour work week, and welcome a life of enjoyment and freedom that runs on less than 10.

There are two basic ways to accomplish this goal. The first is to create and automate a cash flow large enough to sustain your current lifestyle.[1] This is a great option because it

---

[1] For a detailed explanation of this, read Timothy Ferriss' book *The 4-Hour Workweek: Escape the 9-5, Live Anywhere, and Join the New Rich.*

enables you to travel, buy expensive gadgets, and otherwise live large on less than 4 or 5 hours of work a week. However, eliminating work by automating a cash flow requires upfront capital, a particular type of business expertise, and is not always stable. This brings us to the second, simpler option: reduce expenses to negate the need for so much money. Automating cash flow can be unstable, expensive, and difficult; eliminating expenses is sustainable, practically free, and *incredibly* easy.[2] Using the suggestions in this book you can, without sacrificing comfort or security, begin living a work-free life in no time. We were taught to climb on board the 9-5 plane, just like everyone else, and take off towards retirement. But the plane itself, the entire 9-5 paradigm, is based on the false assumptions that work is both good and necessary. It's neither. The system is broken, and we are unwittingly putting off life because we were told it's necessary. Don't stay on board thinking the plane can be fixed or you can exit later. Get the hell out of there.

---

[2] Although I present automating cash flow and eliminating expenses as separate methods, they can, and if possible should, be used together to create a completely labor-free lifestyle. I am currently developing my own automated, no-labor cash flow and plan to include an easy step-by-step guide for you to do the same in the second edition of this book (assuming it works out).

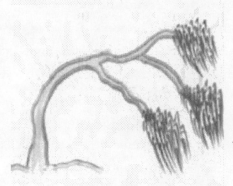

1 Starting Out

If you're like most people, the thought of compiling budgets and financial spreadsheets is comparable to sticking your foot in an ant hill. Unfortunately, in order to spend less you have to have a good handle on where your money is coming from and where it's going. Suffer through these next two exercises so we can get started on the good stuff in the next chapter. You'll be happy you did.

1. Track Expenses for One Month

One of the biggest reasons people are convinced they have to work is that they believe life actually costs what they spend on it. It doesn't, and we often waste a lot of money on things we would do without if it meant we could have more free time. For the next month (and actually do this, start right now), each time you spend any amount of money, even $.25 for a gumball, write it down on a spreadsheet like the example provided. Split expenses which only occur a few times each year (insurance, etc.) into month-sized pieces and add them in as well. You may be shocked to know how much of your money, and therefore time, is invested in things you could easily do without.

List of all expenditures

July

Item	1-Jul	2-Jul	3-Jul	4-Jul	5-Jul	6-Jul	...	31-Jul	Item Total
Gas	25.31								105.2
Batteries			10.98						10.98
Motor Oil			7.25						7.25
Snacks/Drinks		1.5			2.75				12.46
Rent									395
Books									17.5
Groceries	37.18				2.02				127.21
Shoes									24.75
Clothing			9.24						9.24
Eating out					8				35
Donations									22
Electric Bill									23.88
Car Insurance								42	42
Daily Total	62.49	1.5	27.47	0	12.77	0		42	**Monthly Total =** 832.47

2. Make a Budget

You're probably surprised to learn that your daily $1.50 Mountain Dew costs you $45 a month, $540 a year. That's an extra 6 hours of minimum-wage labor per month just to fuel your Dew habit. I'm not trying to suggest that these micro expenses are somehow wrong or even undesirable; if I had the choice between a daily drink or none, I would rather live it up and have the drink. But that's not actually the choice I have to make. The real choice is between a daily drink or an extra six hours to spend however I choose. Personally, I would rather have the latter and use it to go on a picnic with my family.

Using the information you've collected, make a target budget based on week and month increments like the next example. Each time you make a purchase, round up to the nearest dollar and subtract that amount from your budget. Try to stay under target in each category. At the end of the month, keep any leftover funds in that same category for future use. Don't use extra money from one category to fund overdraws from another. When money in one category is gone that's it – you cannot spend more. Eventually, after eliminating some expenses, you will bank enough money to be several months or even a year ahead. After a few years pass and you're secure enough, you can begin providing for your long-term financial needs.

Month of July

	Food $35/wk	Miscellaneous House Expenses $25/mo	Electricity $35/mo	Gas $25/wk	Social Activities $15/wk	Spending Money $35/mo	Emergency money $100/mo
Starting Amount for Month (Already in Bank)	$140	$25	$35	$100	$60	$35	$100
Week of July 1 (expenses)	$25	$5		$24	$8		
	$6				$4		
Balance:	$109	$20	$35	$76	$48	$35	
Week of July 8	35			$22	$9	$7	
					$3		
Balance:	$74	$20	$35	$54	$33	$28	
					$3		
Week of July 15	20		$32	$20	$14		
	2				$2		
	10						
Balance:	$42	$20	$3	$34	$17	$28	
Week of July 22	31	15		$25	$17	$17	
Balance:	$11	$5	$3	$9	$0	$11	$100

2. Living in the Middle

The consumer-driven lifestyle most of us lead is on the far end of the spectrum between environmental consciousness and a complete lack of it, though it doesn't normally seem so because the lifestyle is so common. At the other end of the spectrum are nature-based lifestyles that aim to, as closely as possible, integrate human life with nature. Of the two, the consumer-driven life is the most destructive but the most physically comfortable (for the one living it) while extreme nature-based ones are the least destructive but less comfortable. The trick then, is to find the middle ground where things balance. If everyone in the world consumed as the average American does, we would need 4.1 earths to support us.[3] This is coupled with the fact that we've become accustomed to controlling the outside world, something that, while not inherently bad, can make us feel further removed from the rest of nature. We can create light whenever we wish,

---

[3] Tim De Chant, "If the World's Population Lived Like...". Per Square Mile. August 8, 2012. http://persquaremile.com/2012/08/08/if-the-worlds-population-lived-like/.

change seasons indoors by flipping a switch, and control the harvest times of fruit and vegetables. Unfortunately, all these things come at a price – both to our sense of wellbeing and, too often, to the earth as a whole.

    This discussion is important because the further a lifestyle is removed from the natural world the more effort must be put in to keep it there. Things tend toward their balance point, and that balance point is the way things are outside your home's walls. Put in a more direct way, <u>it's easier to live without certain things than to make the money they require.</u> I hope you will find, as I have, that living between the two extremes of American consumerism and the total rejection of it is a comfortable place to be. I'm not advocating a back-to-nature retreat from modern life; I'm much too fond of hot showers and Netflix for that. But there are ways to have these comforts for little or no cost and cause much less environmental damage. I'll show you how.

3. Fit Into Your Environment, Don't Alter the Environment to Fit You

The former requires less effort. It's as simple as that. Side effects of this overarching philosophy are a more stable mental state, more free time, less environmental damage, and fewer expenses. There are countless ways you can fit into your environment and I've included a few in the tips below to help you get started.

4. Sleep and Wake With the Sun

If you've ever spent extended time outdoors, you know that eventually people begin to get tired when the sun goes down and wake up when it rises again. This natural sunlight-based rhythm helps you fall asleep faster, sleep more soundly, and wake up feeling refreshed. If you have trouble getting up in the mornings, sleep facing an east or south-facing window.

5. Match the Seasons

Another overarching idea that will reduce expenses (and a lot of hassle) is to alter yourself to match to seasons rather than trying to alter the seasons to match you. When we enter climate-controlled rooms or eat food grown out of season, we further remove ourselves from natural processes. Again, the larger the gap between our lives and the world around us, the more effort and money we have to put into keeping it there. Begin with small changes. Sometime this week, meet some friends over coffee and brainstorm ways to alter your lifestyle to fit the seasons and save time and money. Maybe you will decide to eat more season-specific food or let your house warm up a degree or two in the summer and drop a couple of degrees in the winter.

6. Get Rid of Extraneous Amenities

Like TV. Unfortunate, I know. In terms of television alone, a $70 monthly bill requires 9 hours of minimum-wage labor. This may not sound like a lot, but add in your Mountain Dew time (6 hrs) and a dozen or so other luxury expenses, and you'll probably discover that you can work a lot less by going without. How does two weeks off each month sound? Not bad. Instead of watching TV, try reading, playing games, or doing something crafty. This change will save money, develop your intellect, and even help strengthen bonds with your family. A good alternative is to watch free (and legal) TV shows and movies online. www.crackle.com and www.topdocumentaryfilms.com are good options. Remember that the primary motive of television programming is not to entertain, but to sell. Television programming is a conglomeration of businesses that has one primary motive: to make money. Entertainment just happens to be one of the things sold.

There are other reasons to do without the TV as well. For example, advertisers know and capitalize on some sad facts. They know that if a child begs for something long enough most parents eventually give in. They know that most Americans are self-conscious about their bodies and that if a commercial can perpetuate ideas making them feel worse, they are more likely to buy beauty products. Finally, companies know they can sell the idea that the 'good life' requires copious amounts of disposable products; everything from throwaway Keurig coffee cups, to one-use travel-sized toothbrushes, products they profit from.

There are even problems with exaggerated advertising. When I was young, a commercial for a watergun showed the stream of water literally freezing things into blocks of ice. Any adult knows this is an exaggeration and won't think twice about it. However, as a child who didn't understand physics, I thought this marvelous new invention really did what the television showed. So I begged for it. This type of exaggerated advertising is illegal in Canada because it intentionally confuses children. In the United States however, there are no such laws.

7. Meditate

Meditating is a simple way to develop a happier and fuller experience of life. Contrary to most people's impressions, meditation is not some alternative hippie practice, (well… sometimes it is, though not the way I practice) it's an effective way to strengthen your mind and many of its benefits are backed by solid neurological evidence. There are three basic types of meditation: Concentrated, Analytical, and

Visualization. I have taught several applied meditation seminars at East Tennessee State University and guest lectured on meditation for anxiety relief for their nursing program. The best part is that I saw people become more centered and happier during each and every session. For those who continued meditating, the initial effects of calm and happiness became permanent personality traits. Although meditation will not save money (unless you discover something I haven't), the sense of peace it helps develop is still a fundamental part of the good life. I teach concentrated meditation first because it forms a solid foundation that is needed before moving on to analytical and visualization. I will only discuss concentrated meditation here, but I encourage you to explore the other types as well. It's amazing what you can learn to do with your mind.

Practice: For the next week, set a standard time each morning and night for meditation. Five minutes is enough. Set an alarm to let you know when the five minutes are up so you won't be watching the clock when you're supposed to be meditating. Sit cross-legged on the floor, a chair is also fine if you're physically unable. The purpose for sitting a certain way is to learn to associate meditation with a posture so it will be easier to reengage the same mental responses later on. I've found that if I assume a meditative position, my mind tends towards the state it was in the last time I sat that way. This is how our minds work – through associations.

    While sitting cross-legged, fold your hands in front of you (the positioning doesn't really matter). Sit with your back straight but not rigid, and relax. Sitting on a pillow will help straighten your spine. Place a candle or some other object two feet in front of you and focus on it. It's important that there is nothing distracting in your field of vision; this is why I like to teach using a candle in the dark. Breathe deeply into your stomach and give all your attention to the item in front of you. Your mind should be like a fine tuned instrument; not too lax but not too taut either. Breathe deeply and focus. If you're like the rest of us, you'll immediately start thinking about your to-do list or the laundry you've been neglecting. Don't worry or get irritated with yourself, this is how we usually think, jumping from one thing to the next, and so it's understandable why our minds automatically do it. Just calmly refocus on the object in front of you. Repeat this process until the five minutes are up.

    The purpose of concentrated meditation is to hone your ability to remain focused. The average person can only remain totally focused on one thing for 9-10 seconds. Really. But don't worry, this is normal and your ability to focus will improve quickly. During these periods of total immersion you'll experience a deep sense of calm and peace. The more often you engage this state of mind, the more likely it is to show up in your daily interactions. Evolutionarily speaking, our minds are designed to replicate their surroundings to increase our ability to survive in various circumstances. This is the reason your speech patterns change if you spend enough time with a new group of people. Just like your speech, your emotions and state of mind are also affected, and partially determined, by your surroundings. The more often you experience a calm mind, the more likely your mind is to become calm of its own accord outside of meditation time. This will happen automatically, and the only thing you have to do is keep a regular meditation time. The effects are powerful and will greatly improve your interpersonal relationships and feelings of well-being. After a few weeks working with concentrated meditation move on to analytical meditation, an even more powerful way of developing your mind. After a couple of months of analytical training, you can move on to visualization meditation, the most effective type but also one that is ineffective without a strong meditation foundation.

8. Learn Your Land

Foraging for food, medicine, and other resources is cheaper, more sustainable, and much more fulfilling than buying something at a store. But you have to know what's around to use it. I will discuss various foods and medicines you can forage for later, but right now the goal is just to see what's around, even if you don't know what the plants or rocks are. Your house walls already subconsciously separate you from the world outside; reconnect with it by exploring your property or any intact wilderness areas around you. Take along a notepad and jot down any unique or usable resources you find. If you do decide to forage, be careful not to upset the area's balance by removing too much or taking endangered plant species.

9. Don't Buy into Consumer 'Natural'

Companies know that the recent organic, locally grown, and environmentally-friendly movements are mostly confined to middle and upper-middle class families. These people have money. Companies capitalize on this and are mass producing environmentally-friendly products, which would be great, if it were sincere. Because many of these companies are primarily concerned with making money, their 'earth-friendly' products are often packaged in the same plastic as their non-friendly counterparts, and company practices that are out of the consumer's view often remain unchanged. Businesses interested in making money don't employ environmentally-sound practices when they're not profitable, i.e. when they're out of the consumer's eye. While it's true that the more environmentally-friendly something is the cheaper it will be, this does not apply to marked-up consumer products. Doing things yourself and re-envisioning old practices are more sustainable and cost-effective options. If you do decide to purchase profit-motivated products rather than making them yourself, I will say that regardless of who makes the money, products marketed as environmentally-friendly usually cause less overall damage than conventional alternatives.

3 Energy

Electricity is an amazing thing. For what you get, electricity is one of the best investments you can make. However, it's not necessary, and I've been told by several people that life without electricity can be quite fulfilling. But an energy-free lifestyle isn't for me; I like refrigeration, electrical lighting, computers, and all the other great things electricity offers. But the fact remains that I don't like paying for them and have found that you don't always have to.

Heating and Cooling

10. Maximize Direct Insolation

When selecting your home, you should keep in mind how much direct solar radiation (sunlight) it receives. Direct insolation[4] produces free and

---

[4] When I introduce a new term I will explain it in a footnote. Insolation is another term for direct solar radiation. The sunlight must be direct.

natural heat and light, both of which cut down on your energy bill and environmental footprint. As an added bonus, sunlight has been proven to make people feel happier and the radiant heat of the sun feels more comfortable than forced-air heating systems. Select a house or apartment with several glazed surfaces (windows) facing south, where most insolation enters your home. Windows to the north let in little light and are a huge source of heat loss while windows to the east and west fall somewhere in between. As a general rule, multiple south-facing windows, no north-facing ones, and only a few looking east/west is your best option for generating heat and light.

11. Passive Heating

Passive heating and passive solar design are techniques used to capture the sun's warmth and retain it to produce heat with little or no effort from the home owner. Because passive heating is completely free and clean, it is well-suited for an eco-conscious, no-work lifestyle. For a passive system to work, a few criteria must be met. First, you must have *direct* insolation; the sun's rays must strike inside the home or heat storage area. Second, you need a glazed surface, such as a window, to let the sun's rays through while holding the heat inside (think of a closed car during summer). Lastly, there has to be a way to store the heat. Anything with a high potential for mass storage[5] will store heat well. Remember that dark-colored objects absorb more heat than light-colored ones. A concrete floor, any type of masonry, black barrels of water, or even flower pots can work.

A simple passive heating system may look something like this: a house has several south-facing windows with dark-colored stone flooring inside. Because winter sun enters the home from the south, it passes through the windows and is absorbed and stored by the stone. Because the stone holds heat, the house will not heat up too rapidly. Over time, the stone slowly releases heat, while simultaneously storing more as long as the sun strikes it. After the sun goes down, the stone continues to release heat for several hours, the exact amount of time determined by the stone's thickness and how much sunlight it received. Throughout this process the windows trap heat indoors. To help retain the heat, insulating curtains can be closed at night after the heat is gained. Insulated windows perform this insulating function themselves but are expensive

---

[5] This refers to an objects ability to absorb and hold heat. For example, a black piece of wood and a black rock both absorb heat well. However, the rock can hold more heat and will release it evenly over a longer period of time, thus avoiding rapid heating and cooling of the surrounding air. The rock has a higher mass storage potential. This is also called thermal mass.

unless you find them at a salvage yard or demolition site.

12. Don't Waste the Bath Water

The fancy name for this is gray water heat conservation. You invest a lot of money to heat water but receive mere seconds of payback for your investment. Instead of letting that heat flow down the drain, plug your tub while you shower and let the water sit until the next day. It will radiate heat throughout the night, slowly paying you back. If you're able, build a grey water collection system. You can find designs online or develop your own using a collection barrel, piping, or whatever else you can come up with. You will have to clean your bathtub more often if you use the standing water method, but I've found the extra 10 minutes each month worth it.

13. Solar Hot Water

During a recent trip to Nepal, I noticed large black water tanks on the roof of every house. These tanks absorb heat and provide free hot, or on cloudy days warm, water. This is the cheapest way to produce solar hot water (and the least attractive) as black plastic barrels can be bought cheaply or salvaged. A metal 55-gal barrel painted a dark color will also work. I suggest, however, finding more attractive and efficient options, such as building a glass-covered flat metal box to lay flat on your roof. Attach a small storage tank to the top of the box. As the water inside the box heats up, it will flow up into the storage tank while cooler water simultaneously flows down into the heater. Several great DIY designs like this can be found online. Check www.motherearthnews.com to get started. Given a sunny day, these low-cost systems have no problem providing an adequate amount of hot water. On dark or stormy days you may have to supplement with another source.

14. Shade Hot Windows

If heat is your problem, window shades cut down dramatically on daytime heat gain. You can attain a similar effect without losing natural light by building a roof overhang that is long enough to block summer sun but short enough to allow winter sun under. Remember that throughout the year the sun doesn't maintain the same arch in the sky; during the summer it rises higher (meaning the Northern Hemisphere receives more insolation and gains more heat) and during the winter it maintains a lower arch. The further north you are in the northern hemisphere, the lower the winter sun's arch will be. Another option is to use a trellis with deciduous vines as an overhang. These vines shade during the summer and lose their leaves during the winter, allowing maximum light through. A piece of netting is the simplest trellis I can think of and it has the added benefit of being movable. You can even use the super simple, but just as effective, solution of hanging a sheet outside your window. When we lived in Japan, we used a reed window cover. The only problem I had with it, other than having to put it up and take it down every day, was that it cut off a lot of air flow. The last and least effective option is to use curtains inside to block incoming sun. If you go this route, select ones with a light-colored side facing the sun to reflect the hot rays away.

If you go with window overhangs, you need to calculate the depth they need to be for your latitude. Use the formula: $D=L/F$ where $D=$ overhang depth, $L=$ window height, and $F=$ your 'F' factor as indicated in the table. Use the larger F factor number to fully shade windows at noon on June 21 and the smaller one to fully shade until August 1. For example, if you live in Asheville, North Carolina at 35.6°N (you can find your Latitude and Longitude by Googling your city) and want to build an overhang that will shade until August 1, you need to know the height of your windows and the F factor for 35.6°N. For windows four feet tall (48") the equation would be D=48/3, equaling an overhang depth of 10.67". This equation assumes that there is no wall space between the overhang and the top of the windows. If there is, add it to the window height. For more information see www.azsolarcenter.org.

Latitude	F factor
28N	5.6 - 11.1
32N	4.0 - 6.3
36N	3.0 - 4.5
40N	2.5 - 3.4
44N	2.0 - 2.7
48N	1.7 - 2.2
52N	1.5 - 1.8
56N	1.3 - 1.5

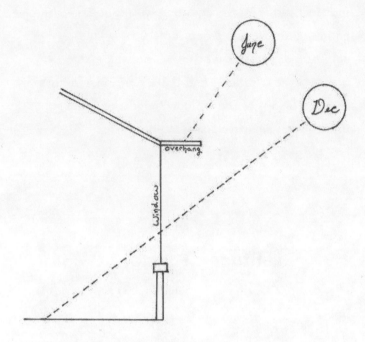

15. Clothing Matters

The cheapest and easiest way to regulate your body temperature is to wear the appropriate clothing. Most people feel they should be able to wear summer clothes indoors even if it is the dead of winter. They can, but they will also pay for it. Wearing thermals, sweat pants, and a jacket indoors during the winter months can reduce or eliminate your need for heating, and thus your heating bill. In the summer, wear fewer clothes or none at all. After all, when you're nude the latest fashions don't seem to matter much anymore!

16. Incorporate Heat from Other Apartments

If you're renting, keep in mind that apartment complexes offer unique opportunities to conserve and generate heat. Walls running between your apartment and others can actually *create* heat rather than simply insulate. Select an apartment that shares walls with others and remember that heat will rise from apartments below and that earth-bermed[6] lower levels almost always regulate temperature better than exposed walls on upper levels.

17. Insulate Winter Windows

Seal your windows shut during the winter months with a crack insulating agent. Insulating strips made for this purpose or strips of old fabric work well.

18. Cook Timely

Do all your cooking at one time to conserve energy. If you can, do the entire week's cooking on the same day and store the food until it's needed. Ovens

---

[6] Earth-bermed shelters use earth piled against their exterior walls to improve temperature regulation. This does not, however, improve the wall's insulating factor. For more information, see the tip on underground housing in the building chapter.

produce a substantial amount of heat which can (and in the winter should) be conserved. In the winter, cook on a particularly cold day rather than a mild one, and in the summer, cook less and leave windows open to lose as much heat as possible.

19. Conserve Dryer Heat

If you use a clothes dryer rather than a laundry line or drying rack, buy a dryer vent diverter box. This $9 switch box connects to your dryer's heat vent and gives you the option of either venting dryer heat outside or diverting it inside to heat your home. The lint trap on the diverter's face will need to be cleaned periodically.

20. The Many Uses of Candles

Candles produce a surprising amount of heat and light, and you can often find them for $.10 or $.20 at yard sales. Most will be paraffin wax candles, a material linked to numerous health problems. Avoid these if you can. I've also heard that frozen candles burn longer but have no idea if it's actually true.

21. Electric Blankets

If you are still cold, try using electric blankets before you turn up the thermostat. They give more effective direct heat rather than heating all the airspace in your home.

22. Why Do Ceiling Fans Turn Both Ways?

In the summer, run ceiling fans counter-clockwise to force air downward. In the winter, slowly run fans clockwise, forcing air up into the heat collected on your ceiling. This will circulate the heat down the periphery of the room.

23. Passive Cooling

Because materials with high thermal mass resist temperature change, they maintain cooler temperatures during warm months the same way they maintain warmer temperatures during cool ones. High thermal mass materials in cool, shaded or underground areas will keep the surrounding air temperature down, helping prevent your home from overheating during the day. Other passive cooling options include painting your roof white (use an actual roof coating, not regular white paint), or covering it with another high-albedo[7] material. High-albedo roof coverings reduce internal temperatures, mitigate the heat island effect,[8] and can be paid for by the government (I will explain how later). On a 1000 ft² house in a warm climate, a white-painted roof can offset approximately 10 tons of CO2 over 20 years by reducing the amount of energy that home needs to run air-conditioning, energy that often comes from dirty (i.e. coal) sources.[9] Earth tubes and cooling towers are also celebrated passive cooling options, but I am not familiar with them. Again, check www.motherearthnews.com for designs.

24. Shade Air-conditioning Units

If you have an outside air-conditioning unit, shade it so it doesn't have to work as hard. Trees offer simultaneous shade and camouflage. Pick deciduous ones so they won't block winter sun.

---

[7] Albedo refers to the ability of a material to reflect sunlight.

[8] Because cities are built with high thermal mass materials, such as concrete and asphalt, they absorb and hold more heat than rural areas. This creates a 'heat island' effect where temperatures in a city typically range 5-10 degrees higher than surrounding areas.

[9] Because high-albedo roof coverings keep buildings cool, they are a good option for hot climates but not for cold ones as they often increase winter heating bills. Check the online calculator at http://web.ornl.gov/sci/roofs+walls/facts/CoolCalcEnergy.htm to see how much money you will save (or lose) by installing one.

25. Avoid the Air Conditioner

According to the U.S. Department of Energy, air conditioning accounts for 54% of the average home's energy bill. Instead of running the A/C, wear fewer clothes, take multiple short, cold showers throughout the day, and keep cold packs in the freezer to put in bed with you at night. You can also create a cheap A/C unit by letting a fan blow over a frozen bottle of water. Lastly, it's surprising how much drinking cold water can affect the way you feel.

26. Turn the Water Heater Down to 120°

Unless you really like to cook when you bathe, 120° will be more than hot enough. 120° is a maximum — try lower temperatures during summer. If you're going to be away for several days, turn the heater all the way down or shut it off. With lower heat settings, you save more energy and less mineral buildup and corrosion occurs, extending the life of your heater. Large tank water heaters can usually be adjusted by removing the control cover plate on the outside of the tank. Hot water tanks are one of the largest energy consumers in the average American household, so they are an easy way to gain substantial energy savings.

27. Wrap the Water Heater

The better insulated your tank is, the more efficient it will be. All water heaters have efficiency ratings such as R-8 and R-9.[10] Heaters with higher numbers are more efficient. If you can't find the heater's efficiency rating on the instruction panel, touch the tank. If it feels warm, it's losing heat. You can buy an insulating jacket from any home improvement store or you can make your own by taping together scrap Fiberglass insulation salvaged from construction sites. Side note: if your energy company charges different rates for peak hour consumption, consider buying a timer and installing it to shut the heater off when appropriate. There are good YouTube videos that can show you how to get one and install it.

28. Wrap Water Heater Piping

This is less effective and more difficult than wrapping the tank itself but still worth considering. Lagging (wrapping) your water heater pipes raises water temperature 2-4 degrees. On top of this, you won't have to wait as long for hot water, saving both water and money while making you more comfortable. If your pipes are too difficult to access, wrap the ones

---

[10] R values are a universal way to designate a material's insulating ability.

within three feet of the heater; these will benefit most from the insulation.

29. Raise Refrigerator and Freezer Settings

Raise the temperature on your refrigerator and freezer as high as they can while still operating effectively.

30. Eliminate Energy Vampires

Appliances left plugged in pull electricity even when they're turned off. The amount normally varies between 2-16 watts each, accounting for 4-5% of the energy used for the average home according to the U.S. Department of Energy. The top energy vampires from top to bottom are: desktop computers, instant on televisions (basically anything with a flat screen), surround sound systems, cable or satellite boxes, and any appliance that keeps time. You can unplug appliances when they're not in use, or a much more convenient option is to connect them to a power strip that can be switched off.

31. One Fixture, One Light bulb

If your fixtures have space for multiple bulbs, only use one or two. In my experience, there is always plenty of light. With this simple tip, even without changing your usage habits, your lighting expenses will be cut in half!

32. LED and CFL bulbs

A compact florescent light bulb (CFL, the swirly ones) uses about 75% less energy than an incandescent bulb, lasts 5 - 7 times longer, and produces 75% less heat. Light Emitting Diodes (LED) bulbs are 17.5% more efficient than CFL's and last 2 - 4 times longer. This means that if you run a single LED bulb 3.5 hours/day, it should last around 41.1 years. Yes, you read that correctly. In addition, LED bulbs are impact resistant, can withstand extreme temperature fluctuations, produce little heat, and do not contain the toxic mercury CFLs do. The main drawback of CFL bulbs is the mercury they contain, an environmentally-damaging and health-hazardous material. This is balanced in some ways by the amount of energy they save compared to incandescents, energy that most likely comes from coal-fired power plants. Because CFLs save so much energy, and energy production actually creates mercury contamination itself, CFLs actually reduce the net amount of mercury introduced into the environment.[11] On the LED side, the main drawback is that many bulbs, though not all, focus light rather than disperse it. Do research to determine which type of LED bulb works best for you. Currently, the cheapest LEDs are $4-$9 and the price is dropping each year.

33. Clean Refrigerator Coils

Refrigerator coils transfer heat from inside your refrigerator to the outside by dispersing it into the surrounding air. When these coils become insulated with dust, they have to work harder to release the heat. Cleaning the coils is easy and should be done at least once per year. Simply vacuum off what you can and remove the rest with a rag. Coils on older refrigerators are connected to the back while newer ones tend to have them behind a toe plate.

---

[11] Energstar.gov, "Mercury Fact Sheet", Energystar.gov, http://www.energystar.gov/ia/partners/promotions/change_light/downloads/Fact_Sheet_Mercury.pdf.

34. Separate the Refrigerator and Stove

Your refrigerator works to keep things cold. Your stove works to keep things hot. Keep adequate distance between them so they don't compete.

35. Keep a Full Freezer

An empty freezer has to work harder to stay cold, so you should pack it as full as possible. If you can't find enough ordinary items, try these unusual alternatives: batteries kept in the freezer have a longer lifespan, 5% longer for alkaline and 90% for nickel-metal hydride; seeds keep longer when cold; and tights frozen after soaking in water are less likely to run. (I actually have no experience with this last one and am skeptical, but it does sound cool.) If you have extra space, fill it with jugs of water.

36. Install Low-flow Showerheads

A low-flow showerhead reduces the amount of water you use and thus your water and water-heating bills. Showerheads with lower gallon per minute (GPM) ratings save more.

37. Install Aerators

Inexpensive aerators ($1-$2) work by mixing air into the water stream from your faucet. As more air equals less water, aerators alter how many gallons per minute your faucet runs. Purchase aerators rated at no more than 1 GPM for maximum efficiency. Be sure to buy ones that fit your faucets; some are threaded differently.

38. Use Water Consciously

Remember Nepal? One house I lived in had very little hot water. As a result, the first person to shower used it all, leaving the rest of us with a nice, refreshing, freezing shower. It didn't take long to learn a more efficient way of bathing. I would turn on the water just long enough to get wet, turn it off while I soaped up, and turn it on once again to rinse off. Nowadays, in my more comfortable house with all the hot water I could want, I (occasionally) still use an incredibly small amount of water and energy using this technique. When doing dishes, instead of filling the sink or running water constantly, scrub and stack dishes on the clean side of the sink and rinse them all at one time. You would be surprised how much water goes down the drain when it's constantly running.

39. Displace Toilet Water

While we're on the subject of water, an easy way to save some is to fill a plastic bottle with water and rocks and place it in your toilet's tank. Each flush will use one less bottle of water.

40. Make Your Own Flow-control Toilet

If you want to go a step beyond displacing toilet water, tie a small weight on top of the stopper inside your toilet's tank. I use a small bolt. The extra weight will close the hole when you release the lever. You just built a flow-control toilet for free! Make sure the weight is not too heavy. If it is, the seal will weaken over time. Alternatively, you can buy and install a dual-flush convertor; it performs a similar function but looks nicer and costs more.

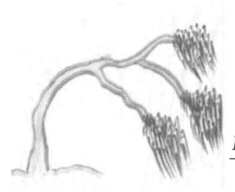

4 Food and Drink

Throughout most of human history, people have spent a lot of time and effort to procure what we can now get for next to nothing. Just think about it; how much time do you actually spend to secure food for the week? Now imagine having to spend upwards of eight hours a day to have a diet that's always based around the same food stuffs. It's a big difference. However, although food doesn't require as much work as it once did, your grocery bill undoubtedly remains a significant expense. It doesn't have to be. My partner and I frequently eat 80% organic for less than $5 per week. We don't skimp on the luxuries either and no, we don't grow all of our own food (too much work). Contrary to popular myth, a healthy diet is the cheapest option. Prepackaged foods seem cheaper when placed next to their mass-produced healthy counterparts, but they're vastly more expensive than the true healthy and environmental options. The tips below will help you eat a healthier, cheaper diet. After all, a better diet now may mean more comfort and fewer medical expenses in the future.

Drink

41. *Water*

Don't drink sodas. They're packed with sugar and wrapped in trash. Teas and juices are better, but still cost money unless you forage for them yourself. Water, on the other hand, is either free or close to it. Stay away from the bottled variety, there's literally no good reason to drink that stuff.[12] Although most people think so, flavored drinks are not a necessity; they're a luxury. An expensive one. Right now, before you read any further, calculate how much you spend each year on flavored drinks and decide if they're worth it to you. Two $1.50 drinks a day cost $1,095/yr, and, hold onto your seat, that $4.95 coffee you get from Starbucks on your way to work each morning costs you another $1,287/yr. To put this into perspective, if you refrained from buying Starbucks and soft drinks for one year you could buy two quality used cars and give them to random families in need. Bam, you

---

[12] 1) It's expensive. 2) Plastic bottles leach chemicals into the water and have been linked to various health problems, especially when they've been exposed to sunlight. 3) Many brands, including the two largest, Aquafina and Dasani, have been shown to be indistinguishable from tap water in purity. They are sourced from "municipal sources", the same place your tap water is, but when the company distills or deionizes the water it can be relabeled as 'purified' instead. 4) Bottles require energy, creating pollution, to produce. 5) Bottles are trash. 6) Did I mention it's expensive?

made a huge difference and a life-long impression on a lot of people. I should know; when I was a child, a random stranger gave me and my family a car when we really needed it. It made an impression. From an environmental point of view, the choice is a little easier to make. According to the U.S. National Park Service, it takes a minimum of 450 years for a plastic bottle to decompose. Of course most of these bottles, the ones that aren't recycled or find their way into water systems, are deposited into landfills where being surrounded by other trash greatly extends the decomposition timeline. PET (recycle code 1) bottles don't biodegrade at all; they break down through a process called photodegradation. This requires direct light, light most bottles won't see when packed into a landfill.

42. Filter, Not Bottles

Bottled water is thousands of times more expensive than tap water and although plastic bottles can be recycled, the recycling process still produces pollution. As an added unfortunate circumstance, people feel better about buying recyclable containers simply because they're recyclable. This means that people buy more plastic because it can be recycled, regardless of whether they actually recycle it or not. The vast majority of purchased bottles are virgin plastic, meaning they are not made from recycled plastic. Have you ever heard of the Great Pacific Garbage Patch? Scary stuff. Sidestep these problems by using a water filter pitcher. The cheapest of these filters, and they can be quite cheap, is equivalent to 300 plastic bottles.

43. Get a Reusable Water Bottle

Do it for the same reasons listed above. Buy a BPA free one. If you like cool water, buy a light-colored insulated bottle; it will reflect more heat than it absorbs.

44. Reuse Tea Bags

Water is wonderful, most of the time, but it can get really boring. I love teas and have found that the stronger the tea is, the more times the leaves or bags can be used. Simply dry the bags on a drying rack and when you make the next pot, throw them in with one fresh bag.

45. Cut Milk and Juice

Extend milk and juice by cutting them with water. It sounds gross, but watered-down milk and juice tastes similar to lighter options; the flavor stays the same. When cooking, use plain water instead of milk whenever possible. Although it may seem obvious, diluting milk or juice 1 to 1 with water will make them last twice as long. Find a balance point that works for you; in many cases you won't notice the difference.

46. Homemade Wine

You can make wine out of various things, but fruit with high water content is the easiest. Squash the fruit into a large glass bottle and add a 1/2 cup of sugar and a pinch of yeast. Shake, cover the opening with a balloon, and store in a dark place. The balloon will blow up and recede when the fermentation is completed. This will take a month or so. Shake the contents once a day, and make sure the opening remains clear. When fermentation stops, strain out the fruit material, top the bottle with water, and let it sit until any residual material settles. Decant.[13] If you and I have similar tastes, you may want to add a touch of honey, vanilla, or some more sugar. MAKE SURE the bottle is finished fermenting before you cap it. I've blown the caps off of two bottles because they continued to ferment just a little bit after I bottled them. Showering the room with wine is not a good way to make you, or your partner, very happy.

---

[13] Siphon out the liquid leaving the residue at the bottom.

Food

47. *Vegetarianism?*

The word vegetarian is problematic and I hate it. It's problematic because it sets up a strict, and thus restrictive, dichotomy between those who eat meat and those who eat none at all. Black and white ways of viewing the world like this are not only fallacious, but they force people to 'choose a side'. This leaves out the middle area and the more accurate question: 'how much meat is best to eat?' I hate the word for the same reason. It's easy to place vegetarians in a category necessarily separate from, and defined in opposition to, 'meat eaters' and thus dismiss most of what they have to say. I'm not advocating vegetarianism because of animal rights (though I think it's a noble cause), rather, in terms of health, expense, and environmental impact a vegetarian diet makes the most sense.[14]

---

[14] There is way too much evidence for this statement to include here. In terms of carbon emissions, water usage, methane emissions, ground water pollution caused by livestock waste, and land space required for production, the environmental choice to eat less meat is obvious. Just in terms of carbon emissions, a study at Carnegie Mellon University found that if a person goes completely vegetarian it would be the equivalent to driving 8,000 fewer miles per year, better than purchasing local food by a long shot. To produce one pound of beef, it takes almost 2,000 gallons of water, and cattle farms are one of the single largest producers of methane, one of the most destructive greenhouse gasses.

Compared to people in most other industrialized nations, Americans eat a lot of meat. This overconsumption, particularly of red meat, is linked to various health issues ranging from heart problems to pancreatic cancer. From a financial standpoint, meat is proportionately the most expensive part of our grocery budget. Cutting your meat consumption, or eliminating it all together, will have an obvious impact on your wallet. In terms of the environment, eating one soy burger instead of a hamburger saves about 579 gallons of water.[15] That's right. You can install all the faucet aerators and low-flow toilets and showerheads you want, but eating one less meat burger per week will blow these other conservation measures out of the water. Lastly, for many of us who are appalled by the disgusting practices of factory farming, it just makes us feel better about ourselves and the rest of the world when we know our lives don't cause the suffering of others. Remember that our food choices directly affect the environment and lives of others. Keep this in mind and eat accordingly; you don't have to consider yourself vegetarian or exclude meat all together.

---

[15] Fisher, Jon. "The Quickest, Easiest Way to Save Water". The Nature Conservancy. October 9, 2012. http://blog.nature.org/conservancy/2012/10/09/the-quickest-easiest-way-to-save-water/.

48. Farmers Markets

There are several reasons to shop at farmers markets: tasting food before you buy, finding local options, and networking, which can lead to co-ops and weekend helpers. Don't be afraid to ask where the food comes from. If the farmer is legitimate (the vast majority are) they'll appreciate your interest. There have been a few cases, however, of the 'farmer' purchasing produce from grocery stores and reselling it as locally grown. Asking where her/his farm is and how the food is grown simultaneously ensures a legitimate product and makes friends. For farms in your area, use the market locator at www.localharvest.org.

49. Buy Apples with Unfamiliar Names

Only the crabapple is native to North America. That said, because other varieties have already become so widespread and our ecosystems have adapted to their presence, the harms normally associated with introducing exotic varieties isn't really a problem when it comes to the apple. A century ago, there were more than 15,000 types of apples in North America, many with striped or spotted skin. Only one fifth of these have survived, and today 81% of those remaining are considered endangered on the marketplace. Over 90% of the apples grown and consumed in the U.S. are from 11 varieties, with good ol' Red Delicious accounting for 40 of those percentage points.[16] The problem is that most consumers like solid-colored, shiny food. Spotted heirloom apples are out and wax-coated Red Delicious are in.[17] Shop at local farmers markets to see what you can find from your area.

50. Buy in Bulk and Freeze, Can, or Dry

When given the option, you should usually buy food in bulk. But check the price per unit first; marketers know people automatically think bulk goods are cheaper and often buy them without checking. If I owned a food company and were interested in making money, I would make the bulk price per unit slightly more expensive to capitalize on shoppers' inattention. Real marketing directors do the same. Some of the best deals can be found at local stores or farmers markets, and you should ask the seller if s/he will cut you a deal if you purchase a lot from them. Believe me, this works almost every time. After you have the food, freeze, can, or dry it.

---

[16] Klemperer, Jerusha. "Apple Varieties Disappear from U.S. Markets". Slow Food U.S.A. November 11, 2010. http://www.slowfoodusa.org/index.php/slow_food/blog_post/apple_varieties_disappear_from_u.s._markets/.

[17] Really, the apples you see in the supermarket are coated in a thin layer of wax so they shine brighter. In the business world, shiny really does equal better.

51. Freeze Food that is Going Bad

Just what the tip says. Old beans, for example, can make killer frozen bean burger patties.

52. Dehydrating and Dehydration Boxes

Sometimes the best way to preserve is to dehydrate. This is especially true if you, like me, are usually short of freezer space. An electric dehydrator is convenient and effective but is only cost efficient if you use it frequently. A cheap alternative is a solar dehydration box. The simplest of these is a four-walled box with a glazed surface on top and small air vents on the bottom and sides. Inside, food is elevated on screens and the entire box is tilted to maximize sun exposure.

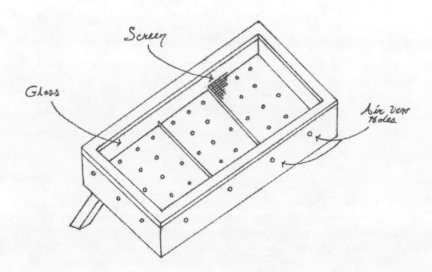

53. How to Dry Apples

Core and slice apples left over at the end of harvest season. I use a hand crank that cores and slices apples into spirals, all in one go. Steam for 5 minutes and dehydrate. They're done when springy. Store in a sealed jar out of direct light. These make wonderful year-round snacks.

54. How to Dry Mushrooms

Separate stems from caps and dehydrate. Store in glass jars. Soak in warm water to reconstitute.

55. How to Dry Herbs

Herbs are easy to grow and just as easy to dry. There are two basic methods: 1) Throw separated leaves into a paper bag, shuffling ever couple of days until dry. The paper wicks away moisture which then evaporates. 2) The easiest method is to hang the entire stem upside down with the leaves still attached. After it dries, a quick pull will knock them off. Store dried herbs in jars out of direct light.

56. How to Pickle

I've never tried pickling myself, but it's many people's favorite preservation technique. The general recipe is: 1) Boil jars and lids in a pot of water to kill bacteria. 2) Loosely pack vegetables in jars. 3) Separately boil 1 part water to 2 parts vinegar and 1 tsp salt per cup. 4) Cover vegetables with the solution, remembering that hot liquids and cold glass do not mix well. 5) Boil jars submerged in water until vegetables are cooked. Seven minutes of boiling will completely kill any bacteria inside the jars, but less time makes crispier veggies. Some things, such as onions and peppers, may not need to be cooked at all. They will be ready to eat in 2 weeks and should keep for 5 months or longer.

57. All You Can Eat for Free

This one is the big one. Americans throw away about 263 million pounds of food each day. A substantial amount of that is thrown by grocery stores and is still edible, only tossed because the sell-by date just passed or will pass within the next week. It's sickening really; perfectly good, packaged food is thrown away every day that won't even pass the sell-by date for several days. Many stores have the policy that if a product will expire before the supply truck returns, it has to be thrown. Produce that is not in an impeccable state is also tossed. After all, people tend to buy the shiniest apple. I'm sure you know where I'm going with this: dumpster diving. It sounds gross, but this is by far the cheapest and most environmentally-sound way of eating I know. Not only are you removing your financial support for transporting food, the trash it's wrapped in, and the harsh chemicals used throughout the production process, but you can actually make a *positive* net effect by recycling the packaging this food is so shamelessly thrown away in and consuming what would otherwise take up space in a landfill. Eating perfectly good dumpster food is free, and by doing so, you're actually making the world a better place.

Truthfully, it's not as disgusting as it sounds. Sometimes dumpster diving is as easy as reaching in and picking up as many organic watermelons as you want. Other times it's not so picturesque. Your first venture will be scary; just get on a bicycle or in your car and drive behind the store. Stop at each dumpster and take a look. If there's anything close enough to grab, reach in and get it. My experience is that within a few trips, people go from timidly reaching in, to jumping in. A surprising number of diverse people dumpster dive for food; I've met everyone from broke college students to serious environmentalists at dumpsters. Although the food is free and will be taken to the dump unless someone eats it, there are others who visit the same dumpsters who may need the food more than you. There's plenty for all, so get what you want but don't clean the place out. I didn't really think about this early on and am sad to remember all the times I carried off all 20 packages of chicken when I knew 5 was all I would eat.

Be careful not to damage anything or make a mess, and always put things back where you found them. As long as there isn't a problem, businesses won't stop divers. They know we're there, but many employees are sympathetic (whether it's because they don't like food waste or because they feel sorry for anyone who eats from dumpsters I don't know, but I've never had a problem). Dumpster diving is a legal grey area; if the business wanted to, theoretically they could charge you with trespassing or even stealing. Although this is a possibility, I've never heard of it actually happening. Learn about the dumping schedule at your local grocery stores, the types of foods they throw, and how long the food keeps after the sell-by/best-by dates. There are a lot of politics behind sell-by dates, and food is often marked with expiration dates *weeks* before it actually goes bad. Companies do this in case something actually does go bad early – better to mark everything conservatively than risk a law suit. Preserve the food by freezing, canning, or drying it.

58. An Important Note

Free things are wonderful—I know; I live off them—but don't take from others when they need it more than you. This applies not only to dumpster food but, more importantly, to the low-income programs and food banks you will undoubtedly qualify for if you live the no-work lifestyle. Don't use them. You are choosing this life and shouldn't expect others to take care of you. Live off society's trash, not its charity.

Another thing to keep in mind is that many others will consider you poor. But poverty is a funny thing; it's always defined in financial terms relative to how much others make regardless of how happy and stable a household is. It's possible to make very little and yet be happy and stable, just as it's possible to make much more and live without either. In the U.S., poverty is defined for most households as earning less than $23,000/yr, much more than what you're likely to make. It's all about being content with what you have; those who earn a lot but are not content will be poorer than those who earn less, but are.

59. The Second Best Thing: Roadkill

No, I'm not joking. You're probably calling me crazy at this point, but hear me out; I assure you my argument is logical. It's the same basic principle as dumpster diving: living off of society's waste is not only free, but it actually improves your community. In this case, by eating animals freshly killed by cars you gain a substantial source of meat that was not factory farmed or involved with any other harmful corporate practice along the way while simultaneously cleaning up and removing the temptation for other animals to venture into the road. This is not as odd as it sounds. Think about it; what's the difference between a dead animal hit in the head by a car and one hit in the head by a hammer at a slaughter house? Where it falls. That's it. Only gather freshly killed meat and jerky it, cook it as normal, or freeze it for later.

The hides can be used to make leather goods. I know a small group of people who subsist off of the leather products they make from roadkill. They really do this. They have virtually no negative impact on the environment, contribute to the local economy, and get to express their artistic side, all with little overhead and nearly 100% profit. You can't get much more sustainable than that. On days they don't feel like working, they don't. Not a bad model. Learn which hides are good for different applications. To skin, hang the body upside down from the ankles and cut a circle around each leg. Then cut a slit from the inside of the hind legs to the anus, down to the throat, around the head, and then back to the slits on the forelegs. Peel off the skin as you would a rubber glove, cutting any residual connective tissue along the way. If this is too sickening for you, I understand; it's on the verge of being too much for me. This is one of the reasons I eat little meat. Otherwise, I would only be okay eating animals if someone else does the killing and preparing—a sad thought.

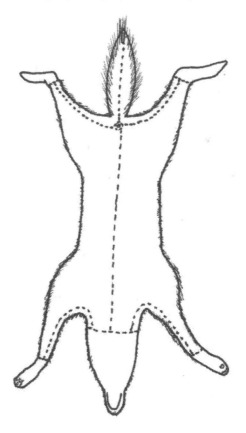

60. How to Tan a Hide

Commercial tanning methods involve harsh, environmentally-destructive and costly chemicals. Luckily, there are still some free and environmentally-sound tanning methods used here in the Appalachian Mountains. The easiest and cheapest method is to: 1) Scrape as much tissue from the hide as possible. 2) Stretch it on a board and tack in place with nails. 3) Salt liberally, making sure to cover the edges. 4) Rub the salt in and change the coating when you think it has pulled as much water as it can. I usually change the first coating after 3 days. 5) Reuse the salt after it dries. 6) After the hide has thoroughly dried, the process usually takes a couple of weeks, rough it up by smacking it over a fence post or railing; the hide will be too stiff to use otherwise. This method will dry the hide with the hair attached. If you don't want the hair, follow the same process but submerge the hide in a bucket filled with water and wood ashes after scraping it. After a few days in the bucket, the hair will pull off easily. This is how old-timers, like my grandfather, used to make banjo heads. Different types of skin behave differently and some are easier to use than others. After you've finished, the hide can be rubbed with a natural oil to increase its plasticity.

61. Forage for Food

Foraging is less sustainable than dumpster diving or eating road kill, but a hell of a lot better than buying from grocery stores. Tread lightly though. Your ecosystem's balance depends on these plants.[18] There's too much information on foraging to include here, but I'll mention a couple of good, widespread plants to look for. I am especially fond of the ones we call 'weeds'. You can also forage for natural medicines, something I'll discuss in more detail later. Whatever you forage for, be sure you know what you're getting. The best idea is to go with an experienced person who can point out plants and talk about their various uses and harvest times. Foraging can be a lot of fun, and I hope you find that the line between work and leisure blurs when you're foraging for mushrooms and bird watching on a cool evening.

62. Dandelion

The great dandelion: so many uses, and so many people who don't know them. You can eat both dandelion flowers and leaves. I recommend eating young leaves as they have a lighter flavor. If you do get older ones, boil them for a couple of minutes to leach the bitterness into the water. Dandelion

---

[18] With the exception of invasive species. You should eat invasive plants first, you'll be doing everything a favor.

flowers have been used to make wine for centuries, and the roots have several purported medicinal applications (I've never tried dandelion medicine and am skeptical as to its effectiveness). Instead of dreading them, learn to appreciate these plants when they grow in your lawn and garden. They're volunteer greens that make wine!

Dandelion

63. Dandelion Wine

This old favorite has been around for a long time and is made basically the same way as other wine. 1) Pick 1 gallon of loosely-packed Dandelion flowers without stems. 2) Cover the flowers with hot water. 3) Close the container and let it sit for 3-4 days, shaking once a day. 4) Strain liquid into a 1 gallon jug and add the juice of 2 oranges, approximately 30oz of sugar, and a couple pinches of yeast. 5) Stir, fill with water, and cap with a balloon. 6) After the fermentation subsides in a few weeks, decant. That's it! If you're not a fan of picking off bugs, gather the flowers in the morning. I will say that I've not had the greatest luck with Dandelion wine because the taste changes so dramatically on a batch by batch basis. I prefer the consistency of fruit wines instead.

64. Pokeweed

Pokeweed is another highly useful plant. In Alabama, where I was born, people eat Poke Sallet where 'Sallet' refers to a cooked vegetable. Unfortunately, many people mispronounce it as 'Poke Salad'. Why unfortunate you ask? Because raw pokeweed is poisonous. You don't have to be afraid though; pokeweed grows *everywhere* and has been eaten for centuries. Young leaves are the tastiest, though the larger, older ones can be eaten as well. The problem is that the leaves are too high in vitamin A. Boil them three times in three different pots of fresh water to make them edible. Use Poke as you would steamed spinach. I particularly like it in lasagnas. Native American Indians used to use the bright purple Poke berries as a dye for their arrow shafts, clothing, and horses. I've even heard you can eat the berries, I know birds do, but you have to catch them at the right time. I have no idea when that right time is. But they do make beautiful homemade ink/dye that my partner and I used on our wedding invitations.

65. How to Make Pokeweed Dye

It's incredibly simple. Collect the berries when plump and deep purple, usually during the end of summer or early fall. You can freeze them for use later and I've never had any go bad if kept frozen. When you're ready to make ink or dye, thaw the berries in a sink full of water and squeeze them into a container. Be careful though; the dye will color almost anything, including the clothes you're wearing. You can dilute the juice with water for a lighter dye, use it as is for ink, or add a small amount of flour if you want it a little thicker.

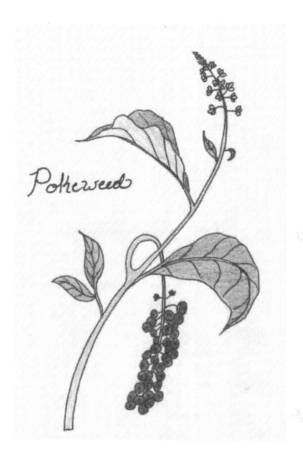

66. Reshi Mushrooms

There are several types of edible mushrooms. There are also a few that can make you seriously ill. Learn the difference. Reshi is an edible variety that has become widespread because they consume dead hemlocks, and thanks to the wooly adelgid, there are now millions of dead hemlocks. A tasty way to cook mushrooms is to separate the soft, outer parts of woody varieties or the stems from caps of other varieties and simmer in a pan with butter. Delicious.

67. Mushroom Tea

Woody mushrooms often have a soft outer part and a hard inner part. After you've separated the soft part to cook, dry, crush, and store the woody leftovers in glass jars. Use like loose leaf tea to extract the mushroom's medicinal benefits.

68. Sassafras Tea

Take the roots of a Sassafras tree, shave off the outer bark, and let dry. The roots are hard to get and require some digging. Because of this, coupled with it's distinct and exotic flavor, I consider this tea a delicacy only for special occasions. Take care not to take too many roots and thereby injure the tree. To make the tea, combine 2 – 4 ounces of shaved root to a quart of boiling water, let it sit for 5 minutes, and strain. At this point, I have to add sugar. I first tried sassafras tea as a child and hated it. Now, I think it's quite good. Maybe this has something to do with developing taste buds, but it could just as easily be that for some things you have to *want* to enjoy the flavor.

69. Other Greens to Forage

Yellow Rocket and Plantains (not the banana-like ones) are also widespread and edible. For more information on foraging and what is available in your area, visit www.eattheweeds.com.

70. Buy From Feed-and-Grain Stores

I have yet to try this (haven't needed to) but have heard it's the way to go when looking for bulk foods. Buy potatoes, wheat, soybeans, and rolled oats from feed-and-grain stores. Tell them it's for human consumption, and they'll help you find a good quality feed. <u>NOTE</u>: I'm not familiar with the differences in food regulation between human and animal feed so do your own research.

71. Glean Food

If the food sources above are not a good fit for you, try this. Gleaning entails gathering (with permission) food left on farms after harvest time. The two basic ways to do this are: 1) Ask local farmers for permission to go through their fields and gather food that was passed-by. 2) Ask neighbors who have fruit-bearing plants if you can pick what's left after they've gathered their fill. If you're feeling froggy, you can even take extra gleaned food and distribute it to the hungry in your community.

72. Buy from Local Markets

Forgo chain stores. They're easy and seem cheap, but supermarket items tend to be exploitative and can actually be more expensive than local options. Look into local and ethnic markets; quality food can often be found cheaper here. For example, there is a small Ethiopian grocer a few miles from my house with a sign so small hardly anyone knows it's there. They sell 25lb bags of rice for $5, one-fifth of the price it is at the supermarket a couple of miles away.

73. Dumpster Dive for Animal Feed

Behind grocery stores you'll find a lot of food not fit for human consumption (or at least not as fit as we're used to), but I've never met another animal who cares. If you keep animals, it only makes sense to feed them with free food. Wear gloves, dumpsters can be gross.

74. TVP

There are some store-bought food stuffs that fit well into a cheap, healthy lifestyle. Textured Vegetable Protein (TVP) is one of them. This dehydrated soy-based protein source is sold by the pack or in bulk by the pound. Buy it by the pound, it's significantly cheaper. TVP is used as a protein source by vegetarians and as a meat extender by many others. Taco Bell, for instance, uses TVP to extend, and thus cheapen, their meat supply. It's light weight, cheap, and healthy. It's also flavorless, so it takes on the flavor of whatever liquid it rehydrates with. Let TVP soak in water until it swells to the consistency you want. One cup of dry TVP makes approximately two cups fully hydrated. We use TVP to make spaghetti sauce, taco meat, and veggie patties. Enough TVP for a month costs us around $6. You can probably find it at a local health food store.

75. Granola

Buy old fashioned rolled oats, not quick oats. There are various ways to make granola. The basic recipe I use is: 1) Mix 3 cups oats, 1/4 tsp salt, and 1/4 cup canola, olive, or vegetable oil. 2) Coat oats evenly. 3) Spread thinly on baking sheet and bake at 300°F. 4) Stir after 15 minutes and continue baking until the oats are light golden brown. For flavor, add honey, cinnamon, vanilla, or brown sugar prior to baking. I like to mix granola with honey-roasted peanuts, chocolate chips, and any bland flavored breakfast cereal for an easy, filling, and energy-packed snack.

76. Make Cornmeal

Corn is easy to grow; all you have to do is plant it and leave it. After you've eaten your fill, store extra ears in a dry location. After a couple of months have passed and it's completely dry, shuck and shell it. Shelling can be done by twisting the cob in your bare hands or by using an old-fashioned hand crank (much faster). The spent cobs make great kindling for wood-burning stoves. Sift the kernels to remove dust and grind with any hand-cranked mill. If it's appropriate for your area, look for a mill at local flea markets before shopping online; you're sure to get a better deal. Homemade meal retains the germ that's removed from commercial cornmeal. Because the germ is the source of flavor, aroma, and vitamins and minerals, commercial meal has to be enriched. The enrichment, however, doesn't replace the taste. Store it in a cool area so the meal's natural oils don't turn rancid.

77. Black Bean Patties

1) Drain and mash 2 cans or an equivalent amount of cooked black beans until most are pureed. Make sure to get out as much water as possible. 2) Mix in 4 tbsp ketchup, 2 tbsp mustard, 2 tsp garlic powder or salt, and 2/3 cup oats. 3) Form into patties and bake on greased pan at 400°F for 7 minutes, flip, and bake 7 minutes longer. Makes around 8 patties. Dry beans are much cheaper than canned ones but take several hours to cook, so plan ahead.

78. Be Creative with Your Food

This is pretty much a requirement. You never know what kind of food you'll find lying around so be creative. Goulashes, stews, and bakes are good ideas or you can mash things up and make 'veggie' patties to freeze for later. Remember that if you're making patties, you need to add a binding agent such as eggs or oatmeal.

79. Try Your Hand at Gardening

Especially for crops that produce a lot of food for little effort. As an added bonus, many can be easily grown organically. You'll find my favorites in the next chapter.

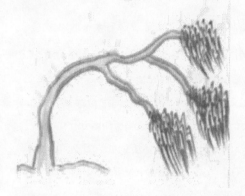

5 Gardening

For me, few things are as satisfying as gardening. Physically working with the land and learning how nature affects things helps us gain valuable insights that span far beyond the garden itself. From an economic point of view, gardening, when done effectively, produces large quantities of cheap, organic produce. You'll have plenty of extra produce, so much that you can give it to neighbors to strengthen ties and encourage reciprocity. Children are amazed when they see the seeds they planted become full-grown plants, and the patience they learn from the process is invaluable. All this said, most people have a difficult time gardening and end up spending dozens of hours only to produce a measly couple baskets of vegetables. The problem usually isn't gardening or their land, it's their methods. Follow the suggestions below and you'll be able to establish a productive, low maintenance garden in one weekend.

80. Gardening Philosophy

Don't 'build' a garden. Remember that our goal is to construct a lifestyle that handles itself and requires less effort from our end. In terms of gardening, this means that our garden should grow by itself, take care of itself, and replant itself. All we need to do is pick the food when it's ready. Impossible, you say? It isn't. Some of the suggestions here directly deal with how to establish a low-maintenance garden while others concern everything from how to get free plants to making natural (and free) insect repellents. The most important thing to keep in mind is that a garden that fits in with the ways and processes of nature will grow without your assistance. Let nature do the work, not your back. If you set up your garden to encourage and capitalize on natural processes, you'll find it requires little attention between planting and harvest. Later, we'll take this same idea, building in accord with nature to reduce or eliminate upkeep, and apply it to housing design as well.

81. How to Get Free Plants

If you had a choice, wouldn't you opt for free trees, shrubs, and flowering plants? Of course you would. Luckily, it's an option. I know of five basic ways to get free plants: 1) When forested or field land is going to be developed, the plants living in that area will most likely be destroyed. Feel free to take small trees, shrubs, and flowers from the area. You should ask first, however. If you're told no, use your own judgment. In many cases these species can be endangered, as was the case when my undergraduate university chose to develop part of its woods system. A faculty member and good friend of mine dug up all the Pink Lady Slippers he could find and transplanted them in his own wooded yard, managing to simultaneously save dozens of endangered plants and populate his yard with beautiful, rare flowers. I feel this is the more ethical choice. 2) You can scavenge plants from landscaped business areas where the business has moved or plant life is overgrown. Again, ask first. 3) Look around on www.freecycle.org for free plants. 4) See if there are any annual tree giveaways where you live. In my area, 10,000 trees of various varieties are given away each year in celebration of Arbor Day. 5) Learn how to propagate trees from cuttings. You can ask and take cuttings directly from wooded areas, neighbor's trees, trees decorating local businesses, or from fruit-producing trees on local farms.

82. How to Take Cuttings and Graft Trees

This isn't my specialty so you'll need to do further research before attempting to propagate via cuttings on your own. What I do know is that cuttings from some types of trees will root by themselves given proper care. Other types of trees can be grafted onto a parent branch or root stock, making the process from cutting to mature plant faster. Growing up, I had a neighbor with a single apple tree that produced three types of apples on three different limbs. Though it isn't very natural, grafting is harmless to the environment and very convenient. Cuttings from woody plants are taken from one year-old growth called scions. They should be taken early in the morning from healthy plants. More information on the various ways to graft trees can be found at Penn State's College of Agricultural Sciences website, www.pubs.cas.psu.edu. More information on rooting can be found at www.ces.ncsu.edu.

83. Micro Gardening in Raised Beds

Most people plant in rows. This requires a lot of upkeep and space. Since most of us have little space and don't want the upkeep, try planting in raised beds constructed from pieces of lumber. Raised beds are less susceptible to weed infestation and growing certain crops in patches is a lot easier to encourage and upkeep than growing them in rows. After all, things tend to grow in patches in nature. Rows? Not so much. Leave the walkways between the beds wide enough to mow if need be. Raised beds are not the best option for everything, but generally speaking, they're much easier to take care of and produce more crop per square foot than traditional row gardening.

84. Strawberries and Used Tires

These two go well together. Strawberries love the radiant-type heat of the sun. Used black tires soak up this heat and re-radiate it later in the day. Plant two or three strawberry plants in a used tire and before you realize it, the plants will spread to fill the entire center. The extra heat enables the plants to produce earlier in the season and to continue producing later.

85. Potatoes

Potatoes are easy to grow and if you never get around to digging them up, it's okay! Potatoes left in the ground from the year before will volunteer new sprouts come spring. There are several ways to store potatoes; if you'll eat them in the next couple of months, the easiest option is to forgo harvesting altogether and dig them up as needed. If it will be a few months before they make it to the dinner table, dig a shallow hole and bury the potatoes one layer at a time with straw in between, covering the top with more soil. The top should be several inches deep to prevent frost damage. This technique has been used for at least the last century and a half here in the mountains.

86. Mushrooms

Mushroom farming is a new love of mine. There are several ways to grow mushrooms, but the most effective method is to inoculate[19] a group of logs and stack them until they start producing, usually during the next spring. The initial investment is small; the simplest outfit only requires a bag of inoculation material (which can be made yourself but is much easier to buy), some wax, a few 6-10 inch diameter logs, and something to drill holes. You can gather the logs from your own land, or if there is a national forest around, you can ask permission and pay a small fee to gather logs from recently cut portions of it. If you do decide to cut your own trees exercise selective cutting, thinning out trees that have grown too close together so the

---

[19] To inject mushroom spores mixed with sawdust, also called spawn, into a predrilled hole in the log.

remaining ones have a better chance of survival. Drill several holes around the outside of the logs and inject them with the inoculation material. An inoculation tool makes this part much easier, but you can do it with only your hands and a stick. Seal the holes by covering them with melted wax and stack the logs in an area out of direct sunlight, preferably an area that receives morning sun but none in the hot afternoon. Mushroom farming requires more effort at the onset than other crops but little after the logs have been inoculated. Each log will produce for two or three years depending on its diameter. It's strangely comforting to pick double handfuls of homegrown, organic mushrooms each week when you haven't worked for them in over a year.

87. Community Gardens

If you don't have enough space for your own garden, see if there are any community gardens around. A park near my house has an area set aside for gardening with individual plots ranging from 300-600 ft^2 and charges an annual $15 fee per plot. Water is included.

88. Compost for the Garden

Compost and manure are excellent fertilizers and should be used instead of synthetic options whenever possible. Composting is easy and a quick online search will turn up various methods of making it. The ideal ratio for compost is 25 parts brown material to every 1 part green. Eyeball this. Brown material is carbon rich and includes dry, dead leaves, wood chips, and pine needles. Green material is nitrogen rich and includes fresh grass clippings and kitchen scraps. Don't try to compost meats, milk, bones, pet waste, butter, or cheese. If you live near a cow pasture, ask the owner if you can gather manure. This should either be free or extremely cheap, (shoot for free, you're doing them a favor).

89. Become Acquainted with the Dump

And see if it offers free fire wood or garden mulch. Many do. Just make the 30 second call and ask; the worst they can say is no.

90. Learn What to Plant Together

Your plants should help each other grow. Although this isn't a magical solution to gardening, companion planting can make your work much easier. The following combinations I know work well: 1) Always plant beans, corn, and squash together. American Indians called these crops the three sisters because they thrive when planted together. Corn stalks provide a pole for beans to climb (this saves *a lot* of time after harvest when you don't have to worry about tangled string and wire), beans fix nitrogen in the soil for the corn, bean vines help stabilize corn stalks against wind damage, and the large squash leaves shade emerging weeds and prevent soil moisture from evaporating. After harvest, the squash decomposes and becomes mulch. 2) Basil improves the growth rate and taste of tomatoes. 3) Plant sun-loving plants around ones which need shade. 4) Group plants with deep and shallow roots together. For a more comprehensive list look around on www.wikipedia.com's page on companion planting.

91. Insect Repellents

Generally speaking, I'm not a fan of insecticides. Killing things simply because they're doing what they do doesn't make me feel very in tune with nature (or like a kind person). Luckily, there are homemade repellents that work well and bypass the issue altogether. Although different types of insects require different repellents, a simple and generally effective catchall is to plant marigolds and garlic sporadically around your garden.

92. Tomato/Potato Leaf Tea Insecticide

If an insecticide is necessary, it's best to stay away from harsh chemicals. Remember that you'll be eating these vegetables eventually, so you shouldn't spray anything you're uncomfortable consuming. Instead, use the toxic leaves of nightshade plants such as tomato, potato, and tobacco to make a deadly solution. Take several potato or tomato leaves (tobacco leaves as well if you just happen to have some around) and rub them between your hands into a bucket of water. Tomato Leaves work best. Let them sit for a day or two and use as a spray.

93. Everything-friendly Insect Traps

These are my favorite forms of insect combat; they cost nothing, are safe, and don't harm the little critters. Here are two effective traps, but there are dozens more out there that work on everything from ants to mice.

Roaches: Lightly grease the inside neck of a milk bottle and fill it with potato shavings or a little stale beer. The food or beer will attract the insects, and they'll be unable to climb back out the greased neck. You can then toss them back outside, far from your house, where they belong.

Fruit Flies: This one is super easy. Put some food in a jar, stale beer works here too, and cover the top with plastic wrap held by a rubber band. Poke several small holes in the plastic. Fruit flies will climb in easily but won't be able to find their way back out. Release the flies outside and reset the trap. This trap can clean out a kitchen full of fruit flies overnight.

94. Weed Killer

Once again (and this is the last time I'll say it, I promise!), stay away from anything with harsh chemicals; they're bad for you, bad for water systems, bad for wildlife, and bad for your wallet. To kill weeds, just pour boiling water on them. That's it. Really. Of course Monsanto (the makers of

Round-Up and a host of other morally questionable agriculture products) doesn't want you to know this. Keep boiling water away from garden plants because you may inadvertently kill them, but it's great for walkways, garden perimeters, and such. You can add 1/2 cup of salt for an extra punch, but boiling water should be fine by itself. Remember that over time, salt use damages soil's ability to produce.

95. Cut Grass Mulch

The next time you cut your grass, let it sit, dry, and use it as a mulch. Shake it well to remove any weed seeds before layering it around. Apply in thin layers so water can still get through easily. Alternatively, you can use leaves. Although leaves can be used whole, if you chop them up more water will be able to seep through. Don't use recycled rubber mulches. The word 'recycled' has mistakenly become synonymous with 'good'. When properly employed, recycling is the lesser of two evils. When it's not properly employed, as in the case of rubber mulches, it's the greater evil. Rubber mulches will not decompose during your lifetime, which means it's going to be around every time you try to do something in your garden. Not to mention it's toxic and smells bad.

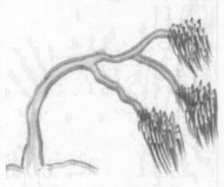

6 Health, Medicine, and Cleaning

This chapter covers a lot of material. Part of this chapter focuses on staying healthy with an aim toward reducing future medical expenses and increasing mobility in old age. In terms of home remedies and cleaning, since introducing too many ingredients at once is fodder for forgetfulness, I have confined the recipes to ones that only use a dozen or so. All but the simplest of these ingredients are included in the following table. A hundred books couldn't contain all the natural/home remedies in use, and I don't have the knowledge to explain most of them. Because of this, I've only included the remedies I'm most familiar with to serve as examples of what can be done with natural medicine. I advocate natural remedies because they have a lighter long-term impact on the body, fewer side effects, and are cheaper than pharmaceuticals. And I just think it's cool to tell people I make my own medicine. As it turns out, becoming a doctor for simple ailments doesn't take that much time if you're reasonably intelligent. Read the top 5 books on natural medicine and you'll have most of the ground work done. The only thing left is to either get guidance from someone who knows their stuff (the best option) or to practice a bit. Of course, the second option takes longer and you should stay away for anything potentially dangerous. All this said, I don't believe natural is the way to go all the time; I become a big baby when I'm sick and eagerly reach for antibiotics if I think I need them. My advice is to use natural options when they are most advantageous and conventional options when they're not. Natural is free and healthy, but conventional is quick and powerful. Lastly, some natural remedies can be dangerous (I didn't include any of these here) and must be prepared by an expert. Before following any of the suggestions below you should, as with most things, research them yourself.

Substance	Relevant Properties
Aloe	Antibacterial, antimicrobial, antiviral, wound healing accelerator, anti-inflammatory.
Basil	Insect deterrent, tastes wonderful
Baking Soda	Cleaning agent
Borax	Cleaning agent, mild toxin if ingested
Garlic	Antibacterial, antiviral, antiseptic, antiparasitic, antiprotozoan, antiviral, antifungal, anthelmintic, immune stimulant, hypotensive, diaphoretic, antispasmodic, cholagogue. An amazing plant. Crush, don't cut.
Honey	Antibiotic, antiviral, anti-inflammatory, anticarcinogenic, expectorant, antiallergenic, antianemic, antifungal, immune stimulant, cell regenerator
Lemon	Antibacterial, antiviral, mild acid
Vodka	Storage medium
White Vinegar	Mild acid, antibacterial, cleaning agent

Health and Home Remedies

96. Alexander Technique

This is super fascinating. As young children we unconsciously learn habits of moving, sitting, and even breathing that conflict with the way our body is naturally constructed. Later in life, these habits can cause health issues ranging from lack of stamina to reoccurring back pain. The solution to all this? Alexander Technique. This method of retraining your body to move in more natural ways was invented by an Australian actor to fix his own problems with a sore throat that would eventually emerge every time he took the stage. Alexander discovered that the cause of his problem was actually the way he stood and held his head while speaking. After retraining his body to align itself correctly, his problem disappeared. Nowadays, Alexander Technique is taught as a means of improving the stamina of actors, musicians, and athletes, increasing mobility in old age, and alleviating certain types of neck and back pain. You can buy books on the subject, but by far the best way to learn is to find a certified Alexander Technique teacher. I can vouch for this; I read an instruction manual first and *thought* I had it, but when I took a class and the teacher moved my head and shoulders where they should be, I *felt* the difference. Books provide knowledge, teachers provide experience.

97. Use Professionals in Training

Students in health and beauty professions need to practice their craft before they can be licensed. Because of this, dental, cosmetology, and various other programs usually offer services for a fraction of the regular cost. All you have to do is call and ask if they take community customers. Students are less experienced than other professionals and normally stick to basic procedures, but there should be instructors available if you or the students have any difficult questions.

98. Geoarbitrage[20] and Medical Tourism

Sometimes products and services are cheaper in other countries. Take advantage of them. Why not combine dental or medical treatment with an extended vacation? You can get quality treatment for 1/3 of the cost in various countries across the globe. Depending on the procedure, the savings could be enough to finance your trip or even add a

---

[20] To use currency and global pricing differences for profit or to obtain cheaper services. For example, instead of hiring an assistant in the U.S. for $8 USD/hr hiring one in India for $4 USD/hr.

little on top! Whether it's dental work in Thailand or knee surgery in Poland, it's often cheaper to get treatment abroad and it's a common practice to do so. The term 'medical tourism' exists for a reason. For more information, see www.wikipedia.org/wiki/Medical_tourism.

99. Take the Stairs and Bike

I've never seen an American woman over 70 riding a bike, but I have seen several Japanese ones. Americans begin losing mobility sooner than their counterparts in other industrialized nations. The reason? One of the main ones is that Americans *expect* to be able to leave their house, immediately get in a car, and drive to the door of their destination. No walking necessary. Japanese, on the other hand, tend to bike or walk comparatively long distances even if they take public transportation. We don't want to get old and fragile too soon, and there are some simple changes that can avoid it. Start by taking the stairs instead of the elevator and biking short distances instead of driving to establish, and maintain, a healthy lifestyle.

100. Let Go of Superfluous Products

I'm not advocating minimalism, but the simple fact is that reducing the number of things we use is the most effective way to reduce expenses, our environmental impact, and exposure to harmful compounds. As I've said *ad nauseum*, the closer your lifestyle matches the way things function naturally, the easier life will be most of the time. You can save a lot of money by deciding to forgo products advertisers try to convince us are necessary, but really aren't. Examples include cologne/perfume (you won't smell bad, I promise), fabric softener (not necessary at all), cosmetics (you're beautiful as you are!), and other hair and beauty products. This might be a hard idea to swallow because these products have become so integrated into our lives that we no longer see them as the unnecessary luxuries they are. Afraid of smelling bad or not looking your best? These fears have been created for us by the people who make money off our insecurities. Don't fall for it. If you do decide to continue using products like these that's fine; make your own or find healthy, cheap alternatives.

101. Be Aware of How You Use Your Time

If you spend 10 minutes on makeup every morning, you'll have spent 1,825 hours over the next 30 years. That's 76 continuous days of prepping.

102. Longer Hair = More Upkeep

And more money. 15 minutes fixing and/or washing your hair every day will be 164,250 minutes over the next 30 years, more than 114 24-hour days of doing nothing but fixing your hair. If you go through 1/2 a bottle of shampoo and one bottle of conditioner a month, a conservative estimate for some people, at $2/bottle, you will spend $1,080 during those same 30 years. Add this to the price and time of your other hair products to see how much your locks cost. I'm not suggesting that you shave your head, but understand that time and expense are proportional to hair length.

103. Stop Shampooing the Normal Way

Regular shampoos clean hair but simultaneously strip away the natural oils that protect and strengthen it. Shampoos contain a byproduct of oil refining, called mineral oil, that lays down a barrier inhibiting your scalp from producing more natural oils. Thus, we need expensive conditioners to mimic the function of the natural oils our body can no longer produce. This is great for capitalism, but not so great for the environment, our wallets, or our heads. Instead, wash your hair with baking soda, 1 tbsp mixed with 1 cup of water. Baking soda is mildly alkaline, so use it if you have naturally oily hair. If you have a dry scalp, try vinegar instead; it has the added benefit of stripping harsh chemicals and balancing the PH level of your head, eliminating any dandruff caused by an imbalance. Neither of these options lather, something that will take a while to get used to. Whether you use regular shampoos or alternative ones, you should shampoo less frequently than most think necessary. Twice each week is plenty. When you first stop using conventional shampoo and start shampooing less frequently, your scalp may overproduce oils. This is a residual response to the mineral oil and should subside in 2 – 4 weeks.

104. Cheap, Eco-friendly Shampoo

If you prefer a shampoo with a little more substance, you can find hundreds of homemade shampoo recipes online. Although many are great environmental options, they can be time consuming to make and a bit expensive. I think the more pragmatic solution is to use the cheapest and easiest portions of homemade recipes to extend store-bought shampoo. First, divide a bottle of regular shampoo into three parts using reused bottles. Use a shampoo that's either unscented or naturally scented so it meshes well with the homemade portion. Make a strong herbal tea (I like peppermint) and dissolve about 3/4 cup borax in it while still hot. Top off the bottles with this mixture. The entire process takes less than five minutes and will cut your shampoo bill by 2/3. Try using this shampoo once every 1-2 weeks and washing with vinegar or baking soda in the interim.

105. Vinegar Dandruff Recipe

If a PH imbalance is the cause of your dandruff, rub vinegar on your scalp and let sit for a few minutes before showering. Shampoo as normal and repeat every 2-3 days.

106. Garlic Dandruff Recipe

What is the most magical food in the world? Surprisingly, it isn't some rare Amazon fruit; it's garlic. Among garlic's many uses is dandruff control. All you have to do is eat a lot of it (though your partner may hate you for it).

107. Crystal Deodorant

Body odor contains pheromones that are instrumental in attracting mates. It's also disgusting stuff (unless it's your loved one's, of course). Store-bought deodorants mask the scent but tend to be expensive and environmentally damaging, they stain our shirts, and are believed to cause cancer. Instead of spending a small fortune on deodorants, try crystal body deodorant made from mineral salt and alum. I highly recommend this, and you can find it in stone, stick, and spray forms. Two years ago, I bought a 5oz rock from the company Crystal. My partner and I use it daily, and it's still 1/3 of its original size. My initial $7 purchase will conceivably last two people 3 years. That's $1.17 per person a year! Right now, calculate how much you spend on deodorant to put this into perspective. Crystal deodorant is fragrance-free, paraben-free, non-sticky, non-staining, leaves no white residue, and can be used by both men and women. Shop for it online or purchase from health food stores. Crystal deodorants are not antiperspirants, but this should be considered a good thing; your pores need to breathe and they absorb whatever chemicals you put on them. On top of this, I've found that by the end of the day I sweat less with deodorant alone than with a deodorant/ antiperspirant. Crystal deodorants work by depositing an invisible layer of mineral salt that kills the bacteria which cause bad smells. Rub it on liberally – the layer is so light you'll never know it's there. It will take two or three days of application for the deodorant to be fully effective, so don't dismay if it doesn't perform to your expectations on the first try.

108. How to Make Homemade Deodorant

If you're looking for a DIY option, mix 1 part baking soda to 1 part cornstarch and add herbs or essential oils for a fresh scent. Some herbs are antibiotic and help eliminate body odor by killing the bacteria that cause it. In order of effectiveness, these herbs are: coriander, licorice, oregano, rosemary, ginger, and nutmeg. Although this recipe works and is super cheap, I remain dissatisfied with it because you need to reapply the powder after 4-6 hours. This is cheaper and healthier than store-bought varieties, but less effective than crystal deodorant.

109. The Cup

The brand DivaCup is the most well-known menstrual cup and although I think this little silicone cup is rashly overpriced, you'll still end up saving money in the long term by using it instead of tampons and pads. The cup will be terrifying at first; putting that thing inside you won't sound like a good idea, but it's safe, easy, and you'll quickly forget it's even there. The cup works by collecting menstrual fluids; all you do is empty the cup when it's full, rinse it out, and put it back in. Expensive tampons and pads (and the trash they produce) are a thing of the past! Depending on your flow, you may need to wear a light pad for extra protection. With the DivaCup or one of the cheaper, newer brands, you also don't have to worry about Toxic Shock Syndrome (TSS) associated with tampons. Whereas you can only leave a tampon in for a few hours, you can technically leave the cup in for days. Oh, and if you think you may start your period soon, you can put the cup in ahead of time. No more unfortunate discoveries.

110. Homemade Cologne and Perfume

Here is the basic recipe my partner uses to make our cologne/perfume, but it can be altered to create hundreds of different scents. Ingredients: 3/4 cup vodka, 1 tsp or 1 teabag rosemary, 14 drops sandalwood essential oil, 7 drops coriander essential oil, 1/4 teaspoon jojoba oil. 1) Make a strong rosemary tea, strain, and add in all other ingredients. 2) Mix and let sit for 1 week. This produces a gentlemanly, woodsy smell. For a sweeter one, try peppermint tea and/or 1/2 tsp vanilla extract or flower essential oil.

111. Natural Hair Dyes

There are several effective natural hair dyes that can be made for little or no money. As an added bonus, they don't damage your hair the way chemically-intensive store-bought dyes do. Paprika, beet juice, and red zinger tea produce reddish tones; ginger, nutmeg, and warm coffee produce brown tones; and Chamomile and lemon juice bring out blonde highlights. Dilute your choice with a little hot water, apply liberally to your hair, and let sun dry. Don't wash your hair for a few days beforehand. Make sure to expose all of your hair to the sun, including the underside. The first time you wash your hair after dying it, do so in water as hot as you can stand. This will help set in the color.

112. Citrus Air Fresheners

Boil leftover lemon or orange peels in a large pot of water, remove from heat, and let sit for a few hours. The peels will release oils that give your home a nice, fresh scent.

113. Vinegar Sunburn Relief

I discovered this on a whim and after looking into it, discovered it's actually a common remedy. Any type of vinegar will work, but apple cider vinegar seems to be the most effective. The acetic acid in vinegar soothes sunburned skin immediately, and numerous old home remedies claim that vinegar will help heal sunburn and reduce or eliminate the peeling process. As far as I can tell, it works. Don't worry about the smell; once vinegar dries it's fragrance-free.

114. Overcoming Allergies

Perhaps the oldest and most well-known allergy remedy is to eat local wildflower honey. Make sure it's wildflower honey and as local as possible. This works because, ideally, bees gather pollen from the same plants that cause your allergies. Eating their honey helps your body develop immunities.

115. Old Mountain Cold remedy

When I was a child, this was my grandfather's cure for the common cold. Take a swig of a strong shine (moonshine, though I suppose any strong liquor would work) and lay in bed under every blanket you can find. This forces you to sweat, a lot, ridding the body of toxins. My mother would have thrown a fit if she caught me drinking moonshine as a child (and probably still would), so I can't personally attest to this remedy's effectiveness. I do know, however, that people have used it for generations.

116. Honey and Garlic Sore Throat Syrup

I like the taste. My partner won't touch it. In a sauce pan, crush and simmer a couple bulbs of garlic in just enough water to cover. Mix the liquid 1 to 1 with honey, and take several teaspoons before bed. This is effective because both the honey and garlic kill bacteria and viruses while the honey lays down a protective coating over the throat, easing the scratchy feeling.

117. Spicy Flu Tea

Ingredients: 1 tsp cinnamon, 1 tsp powdered ginger or echinacea, and 6 cardamom seeds. Cover ingredients in 2 cups boiling water and let steep for 20 minutes. As a general rule, let medicinal teas steep longer than regular tea so the ingredients can release their properties. Cinnamon kills viruses, ginger relieves nausea, echinacea boosts the immune system, and cardamom reduces body aches.

118. Drink Herbal Teas

For overall health and good feelings. For example, catnip tea acts as a sedative, lavender tea relaxes and sedates, while chamomile calms and relaxes. I've included a table with some common herbs for use in both teas and other medical applications.

Herb	Part Used	Relevant Properties
Cardamom	Seed	Antibacterial, pain reliever, antispasmodic (relives stomach cramps, nausea and morning sickness)
Catnip	Leaf	Mild sedative, insect deterrent
Chamomile	Flower	Mild sedative, anti-inflammatory
Echinacea	Flower, Root	Immune stimulant, anti-inflammatory, antibacterial
Ginger	Root	Antibacterial, antiviral, circulatory stimulant, relieves nausea, blood thinner
Lavender	Flower	Mild sedative
Peppermint	Leaf	Antispasmodic (relieves nausea, gas, and bloating), pain reliever, antifungal, expels mucus, fever reducer, insect repellent, stimulant, vasoconstrictor (relieves headaches)
Queen Anne's Lace	Seed	Abortifacient
Rosemary	Leaf	Antibacterial, antidepressant, anti-inflammatory
Thyme	Leaf	Expels mucus, calms cough impulse, settles stomach, and relieves aches

119. Some Remedies are Environmental

Our problems are sometimes caused by external factors rather than internal ones. For example, if you have trouble waking up in the morning it could be because of a lack of sunlight, decreased oxygen levels in the room caused by breathing in an enclosed space, temperatures that are too hot, or not enough room to sleep comfortably. Solve the problems by changing your environment; open a window, sleep facing the sun, and spread out.

120. Aloe for Burns

Aloe is probably the best burn remedy in existence. Immediately after being burned, liberally apply aloe leaf juice to the affected area. Reapply often. You can substitute honey if you have no aloe, but it will be less effective. Don't cover the burn unless you have to. If you must, use a loose cloth bandage and change it frequently. Cloths without harsh dyes are preferable.

121. Chamomile Burn Remedy

If you don't have aloe or honey, chamomile tea bags can be used. Dip the fresh bag in cold water and apply as a compress.

122. Basil for Bee Stings

I always keep basil in my garden; it grows like crazy, has several uses, and makes me feel better when my other plants don't do so well. If you're stung by a bee, briefly chew a fresh leaf and press on the sting site to relieve the pain. Old-timers here in the mountains still do this with chewing tobacco. I was shocked and a little grossed out the first time someone did this to me, though I will say it worked well.

123. Basil Mosquito Repellent

Basil is an excellent mosquito repellent. Use a potted plant, a dry rub, or steep it in water and use as a spray. To make the spray, boil a handful of leaves in a cup of water and let steep for 1-2 hours. Longer is better. Strain and add the liquid to an equal amount of vodka.

124. Catnip Mosquito Repellent

Use like basil. I've read articles (can't find any peer-reviewed ones though) that claim it's up to 10 times stronger than DEET. Pro: unlike DEET, catnip doesn't kill all the birds. And yes, your kitties will love it.

125. Garlic Flea Repellent

Solve the flea problem before it begins by feeding your pet garlic; fleas hate it. Some sources say that large amounts of garlic (around 50 cloves for a mid-sized dog) or using it long-term can be unhealthy for animals. I've never heard of anyone having a problem, but you should look into it yourself.

126. Borax Insecticide

One of the best natural insecticides, even for roaches, is plain borax. The smell of borax alone will drive some bugs away while the ones who eat it die quickly. Sprinkle a little in cabinets and in areas bugs can come in. Renew every 6 months or so. If you're set on killing all of them, mix the borax with granulated sugar or syrup, this will encourage them to eat it.

127. Natural Contraceptives

A man once told me that his grandmother, an old mountain woman, told him he was around because she didn't have her seeds. Of course, neither of us knew what she was talking about. Luckily, however, a local professor who specializes in Appalachian medicine did. She was talking about Queen Anne's Lace (QAL) seeds, a contraceptive that has been used effectively for centuries and is making a comeback. QAL grows almost everywhere and is easy to spot. Now, thousands of couples are using it as a primary birth control method. When this remedy was still common, women kept the knowledge of it amongst themselves and generations of men have grown and died without knowing their wives used it. The primary reason for this secrecy is that QAL was a way for women to retain some control over reproduction in a culture that officially gave it all to men. By using natural contraceptives, women could decide whether or not they had to endure pregnancy, birth, and childrearing.

    Try this at your own risk and only after further research. Collect the seeds in fall and store in dark glass containers away from light. Within 12 hours of coitus (penis/vaginal intercourse) thoroughly chew a teaspoon of seeds and swallow with water or juice. Chewing is important because the seeds release oils when chewed that prevent the egg from implanting. One teaspoon is the recommended amount for a woman of average height and build; larger women may want to increase the dose. Suggestions for how long to continue eating the seeds varies: some say immediately following intercourse or once the morning after is sufficient while others say to continue taking the seeds once per day for the following week. Some people even use QAL as a regular form of birth control by taking the seeds daily or throughout their fertile time. QAL can even be used with pets, though I could not find any controlled studies on the subject. Wild Yam is another, perhaps more effective, herbal contraceptive but one I know less about. The site www.sisterzeus.com is an excellent source of information. It's not academic, however, and any information found there should be verified by another, credible source.

128. Try a Natural Abortion First

Don't freak out just yet. Natural abortions have been performed for thousands of years and have, as far as we can tell, *always* been a part of human society. Done properly, they are also safe (probably safer than using cancer-causing vinyl shower curtains, but more on this later). My suggestion is that if you plan to have a clinical abortion you should consider natural options first; they are often effective in-and-of themselves and, as they cost little or nothing, can save a lot of money. There are both herbal and extractive options. Herbal options usually take at least two weeks of treatment and, should they fail, you need to continue with a clinical abortion or risk birth defects. For this reason, <u>make sure</u> your two weeks of natural treatment will finish well before the legal time limit for a clinical abortion. Also be aware that most herbal options must be completed within 8 weeks of conception.

Extractive options, like menstrual extraction, are much faster. Several herbal abortifacients, as well as menstrual extraction, have solid track records, but you must first be aware of the risks and restrictions involved with them. Educate yourself well. More information and various options can be found at www.sisterzeus.com. Again, try at your own risk.

Cleaning and Laundry

129. Beware Things that Smell

This one doesn't really save money up front, but may pay off in the long term. As sad as it is, if something smells and you bought it from a store, it's probably bad for you. In the U.S. the chemicals used in certain industries, including cosmetics and air fresheners, are not as heavily regulated as they are in other countries. Because of this, many of these products contain chemicals known to cause serious health problems. Phthalates found in nail polish and synthetic fragrances, for example, have been linked to early puberty in girls, a risk factor for breast cancer later in life.[21] Flame retardants used in cars and carpets are loaded with Volatile Organic Compounds (VOCs). Studies have shown that VOCs cause health issues ranging from cancer to headaches and birth defects. Trapping yourself and your family in an enclosed space with these chemicals is not a good decision. Unfortunately, most of us don't know what these smells are and,

---

[21] For more information on cosmetic ingredients see www.cosmeticdatabase.com. Produced by a nonprofit group of scientists called the Environmental Working Group, this site lists data on over 20,000 cosmetic and health products. Look up your current brands and compare them to others on the site.

even when we start having chronic headaches in our 30's and 40's, still don't make the connection. Remember that a healthier life now means fewer health problems in the future. Fewer health problems means more days of relaxing and adventure.

130. Don't Wash too Soon

How often do you wash your pants? If you said more than once a week and they're not covered in dirt, it's too much. Wait until they *need* to be washed. Really think about it; does that pair of shorts really need to be washed after every wear? When you wash clothes too often they wear out sooner, use more water, energy, and your time.

131. Soap Nuts

Soap nuts are dried fruit that can be used to wash clothes. Even though they've recently exploded in popularity, they have been used for thousands of years. Tie a few in a little bag and throw it in with your laundry. Each nut can be reused several times, reducing each wash to pennies even when the nuts are purchased from over-priced retailers. You'll find them cheaper online than in brick and mortar stores.

132. Ultra-concentrated, Biodegradable Detergent

This is what we use. I've found that even though you can almost always make your own products, many can be bought so cheaply that the extra time and effort to make them yourself just isn't justifiable. Laundry detergent is one of these. Buy ultra-concentrated to save money and use less plastic. Make sure the detergent is biodegradable; it's a shame to see sudsy grey water in our streams and an even bigger shame to know how many fish it kills on a regular basis. My partner and I go through one 100oz bottle of detergent every two *years*. No, I'm not joking and yes, we keep our clothes clean. Remember, how much something costs initially isn't important; look into how much it will cost over the life of the product.

133. Homemade Laundry Detergent

I don't fool with this because, using the tips above, I only spend $1.50 or so per year on detergent. But if you feel so inclined, a cheap, easy, and safe alternative is to mix 1 cup borax, 1 cup baking soda, and 1 bar shaved soap. Use 2 tbs per load.

134. Hang Dry Clothes

This is easier during warm months. The benefits are obvious; less electricity use and less heat created indoors are the big ones. When the clothes are almost dry, throw them in an electric dryer for a few minutes to finish the drying process and remove wrinkles.

135. Make Your Own Clothes Washer

Cut a small hole in the lid of a 5 gallon bucket. You can salvage these from construction sites. Cut three small holes in a plunger and it place into the bucket, feeding handle through the hole in the lid. Put in some water, a little detergent, and a few shirts or a pair of pants. Close the lid and plunge away.

136. Wash in Cold water

Hot water sets in stains and requires energy. Cold water will clean your clothes just fine; it's all I've ever used.

137. Ultra-concentrated Dish Soap[22]

I use store-bought, ultra-concentrated dish soap and have been using the same 24oz bottle of Dawn for the past 2 1/2 years. Don't squeeze soap into a sink full of water or you'll go through a bottle a month. Drop a single drop into a jar half-full of water and shake vigorously. Apply the suds to a rag or sponge; one or two drops should do an average-sized load of dishes.

138. Cheap, Eco-friendly Dish Soap

To make your own, mix 1 3/4 cups boiling water, 1 tbsp borax, and 1 tbsp grated soap. Castile soap is a good choice. Mix thoroughly and let sit for a few hours. The mixture will solidify slightly after cooling.

139. Use Less than You Think Necessary

This includes laundry detergent, toothpaste, dish soap, and shampoo. Use at most half the recommended amount of laundry detergent – it will be plenty. Play around with the amount; you'll find that sometimes, no matter how much detergent you use, you really can't tell a difference in your clothes. Think, 'What does this mean?' Using too much

---

[22] If you eat vegan, dish soap isn't actually necessary at all. Aside from removing grease, soap is used to kill bacteria like Salmonella and Campylobacter, something you don't have to worry about if you avoid meat and dairy products.

detergent doesn't really make your clothes cleaner; it can trap dirt inside the fabric. Use 1/4 the amount of toothpaste you think is necessary. Use less shampoo and instead of leaving it in the bottles it comes in, put shampoo in an old hand soap pump bottle. Think about it; if you were a shampoo manufacturer and selling more bottles was your primary concern, how would you do it? An easy solution would be to make the hole on top 20% larger than it needs to be. This way consumers spill out 20% more and must purchase their next bottle sooner. Easy change, more profit. Real companies do the same thing. Putting shampoo in a pump bottle makes it easier to use less.

140. Homemade Toothpaste

Dissolve 2/3 cup baking soda and 4 tsp sea salt in enough water to make a paste. This does not provide fluoride, but this is a good thing according to some studies that show fluoride is toxic and can cause various health problems. You can add your favorite herbs, peppermint for example, to flavor the paste. Certain herbs such as sage can also be added for their antimicrobial properties. Coconut oil will thicken the mix and give some extra tooth decay prevention. If you do decide to stick with store-bought toothpaste consider Desert Essence, Tom's of Maine, or Natures Gate. They're expensive but don't test on animals whereas Crest and Rembrandt do.[23]

141. Tube Squeezer

I have a nifty little tool that squeezes every speck of toothpaste out of a tube. But this tip is actually more about using everything possible and not throwing anything away before its time, whether it's toothpaste, clothing, or even pieces of scrap paper.

---

[23] Another large company, Colgate, still tests on animals but has been recognized by PETA under their new "Working of Regulatory Change" category for only testing on animals when it is government mandated and actively seeking more humane alternatives.

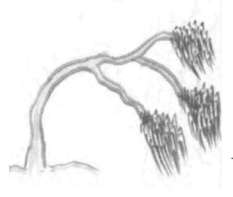

7 Clothing and Stuff

So far we've covered numerous ways to save money, and therefore time, by reducing expenses through eco-friendly changes. The focus of this chapter is how to supply our material wants for free or close to it, and how to make each purchase go further. There are several ways to get free stuff, everything from flat screen TVs to kitchen appliances and books. I will explain how here. When you do have to actually buy something, it's almost always better to spend more money once on a quality item than spending less money multiple times on short-lived, cheap ones.

142. Get Free Stuff Online

You can get everything from books to washing machines for free if you know where to look. There are two ways to get free stuff online: swap sites and free sites. On swap sites you trade one item for another, normally a book or something similar. My top swap sites are: www.DigNswap.com, www.paperbackswap.com, www.swaptrees.com, and www.swapitgreen.com. Stuff on free sites are, well, free. My top free sites are: the 'free' section of www.craigslist.org and www.freecycle.org. I am a big proponent of freecycle, a grassroots movement of people helping people while keeping perfectly good, but unwanted items out of landfills.

143. *Free eBooks*

You can also find hundreds of free eBooks on Kindle, and other electronic book platforms. Openculture.com has an extensive listing of free eBooks that includes every classic I can think of from Vergil's *Aeneid* to Tolstoy's *Anna Karenina*. This is especially convenient if you or your children need a classic for a school project. If you don't have an e-reader, I suggest Amazon's Kindle with an E ink pearl screen (not the backlit kind, they're uncomfortable to read for long periods). You can get a used 2nd or 3rd generation one on ebay for around $40.

144. Practice Haggling, It Will Pay Off

Chances are you've never walked into a store with set prices and asked the casher for a discount. I would like to change that. You can haggle almost everywhere, from local markets to large chain stores, and while most Americans aren't used to it, it's common practice around most of the world. Haggling is a skill, and you will get better at it with time. While it can be done almost everywhere, it's definitely easiest at locally-owned businesses or markets where the person selling the goods has control over either the product's price, or coupons and other discounts. It's a good idea to start small, perhaps at a local flea or farmers market, where you can practice tact and technique.

So, this leads into my challenge for you: Take $50, $50 only, and go to a market or local store. Gather $75 worth of items, usually several small items is easier than one large one. Your goal is to get the price at or below $50. Ask, "Can you give a discount?" or "Can you go any lower?" to let the seller negotiate against him/herself first. Make sure you say things like *'Can* you go any lower?' rather than 'Is that your lowest price?' The latter suggests you are willing to pay the original sum. After a little bit of back and forth, make a firm offer at your target. If they refuse, thank them and walk away. This exercise does two things. First, it teaches haggling technique. Second, it gets you comfortable walking away, something a good negotiator must know how to do.

If you want to haggle over an individual item, you can also begin by asking the price and following with "Can you go any lower?" or something similar just like before. After they give their new lowest price[24] politely offer a price below what you are willing to pay. This is called bracketing. For example, on a $200 advertising campaign you want for $150, offer $125. They will counter with $175, at which time you offer to split the difference and arrive at $150 – your target. When you make your last offer, make it firm. If it's turned down, thank them and walk away.[25] I've found that about 1/3 of the time the seller will stop me and accept my offer. Another technique that works well is to make the seller second guess themselves. When they quote a price, act shocked and say something like, "Way too

---

[24] If it doesn't change ask, "Have you ever made an exception?" If they've made an exception in the past, and are honest, they will feel compelled to bargain with you.

[25] If applicable, give them your card and tell them to call if they change their mind. People don't like it when money walks out the door and will often call and accept your offer a couple of days later. Expect to wait for at least two days; no one wants to seem weak by giving in the day of and a couple of days gives the seller time to decide s/he needs the money.

high!"[26] Occasionally, the seller will immediately start negotiating, giving you a lower price. After you're comfortable, don't be afraid to haggle for more expensive things; even doctors can sometimes find cheaper ways to work on you if they're prompted in an appropriate manner.

145. Threaten People

Call your TV, phone, or internet service provider and politely ask them to drop your service. If you feel like it, add something about how it's just a little bit too expensive. These companies have customer retention departments for a reason and will often offer a better rate to keep your checks coming in. It's much more difficult to get a new customer than to keep one you already have – they've already invested time and effort into you and they know it. It's just bad business to let you go. My friend Abby recently tried to drop her cell phone service only to be offered a significantly reduced bill if she stayed on. She took it. Only try this if you're confident you can pull back if they don't take the bait.

---

[26] This technique is best used when getting quotes for contracted labor.

146. Offer Your Body...Or Skills

If you have a talent or skill, offer it in exchange for items or services. I was a ballroom dance instructor in college and have taught couples in exchange for various services. Brainstorm 1) what you want, and 2) what skills you have to offer. Look at your CV/resume creatively. I also have a love for languages and during undergrad would trade international students an hour of English paper editing for an hour of language instruction. I studied Nepali, Punjabi, and Chinese using methods like this. Of course, you can trade more than just your skills. I also met a lot of art students who needed live models for their work, and though they were always broke, they were willing to trade home-cooked dinners and finished pieces of art if I sat for them. Sit for an hour and get a cool painting and meal. Not bad.

147. Thrift Stores: The Best Choice

Shopping in thrift stores is almost always the most environmentally-friendly option. The production of new goods, regardless of how environmentally-friendly that production is, is still more damaging that using what already exists. Pick a store that supports a cause you like. For example, a friend of mine owns a thrift store that donates thousands of dollars each month to local animal shelters. You'll find that children's clothing is plentiful and I strongly suggest you don't buy it new; children grow too quickly. Adult clothing, furniture, and shoes are other good thrift store products.

148. Free TV's and Mini Refrigerators

Every Fall college students move into dorms, and every spring they move out again. When they move in, students buy a bunch of new 'college' stuff like bookshelves, mini refrigerators, and desk chairs. When they move out, without fail, they discover that there isn't enough room in their car to get everything home. So what do they do? Throw stuff away. This is where we come in. At the end of move out week in Late April/early May, take a tour of dorm and nearby apartment dumpsters. Most of the stuff tossed is less than two semesters old and there is a lot of it. Just like diving for food, check your local laws; this may be illegal in your area (though again I've never heard of anyone caring). This year beside a single dumpster I found a couch, TV/VCR combo, desk, new kitchen utensils and baking pans, oil paintings, 3 lamps, and 2 microwaves, all in good condition.

149. Estate Auctions

Estate auctions are used to sell people's possessions after they move or die. Their assets are auctioned off to the highest bidder, everything from kitchen mugs to the house and land itself. These auctions are great places to find deals. A few months ago, my friend Katie got a new washer and dryer set for under $100.

150. Never Buy New

Well, almost never. New items both cost more, and use virgin materials. I recently bought a virtually new IPod on Amazon, no signs of being used, for half the cost of a new one. Just be careful when buying used electronics.

151. Shop Online

It seems counter intuitive, but having something trucked to your house usually creates less pollution than driving to get it yourself. Shopping online gives you more options, lower prices, and product reviews.

152. Make Your Own

But only when it is the most pragmatic option. Thrift stores and flea markets are usually cheaper and more sustainable.

153. Cloth Heating/Cold Pack

As an example of something that you can make yourself, cut a 16in diameter circle from an old t-shirt. Fill the center with rice and some soothing herbs or essential oil. Gather the circle's edges together and tie with a string. Remember to finish your knots with a simple overhand knot to lock it in place. These bags can be kept in a freezer to use as cold packs or heated in a microwave.

154. Make Your Children's Toys

Whether it's play dough, rubber band guns, or building blocks, if you make your own toys a few things happen: 1) You'll know what is in it and are thus able to keep harmful chemicals away from your children. 2) It's cheaper compared to the toy's store-bought equivalent. 3) You will develop a sense of pride and new connection to your child's life. In their later years, children will appreciate a toy you made more anyway.

155. Homemade Play Dough

Ingredients: 1/2 cup flour, 1/2 cup water, 1/4 cup salt, 1/2 tbsp oil, 1/2 tsp cream of tartar, and food coloring if preferred. Mix ingredients in a saucepan and cook on low heat until it forms a dough. Knead on a floured surface until cool and store in the refrigerator. You can also add texture by mixing in coffee grounds or rolled oats. Kids love it.

156. What Makes a Child Happy

Think about it. Children are like adults; they're generally happier when they have fewer toys than when they have boxes full of them. When they have fewer toys, children stay entertained and use their imaginations and ingenuity to make life fun. When children have boxes full of toys, the 'there's nothing to do' syndrome becomes the norm. Don't worry about giving your kids a fun life, they'll make life fun. On top of this, children who have fewer toys strengthen their imaginations and, I firmly believe, will become more ingenuitive adults. Plus fewer toys means less mess.

157. Learn to Fix Things

Why throw something away if it can be fixed? Be adventurous with your repairs; the item is already broken so it doesn't matter if you break it more. In fact, I have a friend who combines his electronic knowhow with dumpster diving to get multiple free computers and flat screen TVs each year.

158. Look Up, Look Down, Look All Around...

Product placement drives sells. Because shoppers tend to shop at eye level, products with the highest profit margins are usually stocked there. Cheaper items can sometimes be found on higher or lower shelves. This same technique is used to target children by stocking candy and colorful toys on their level. So, we arrive at the unfortunate circumstance that even though you and your children are shopping in the same building, you're experiencing two different stores with two different objectives. Want your child to stop begging for things? Try letting them ride in the cart or on your shoulders. They'll enjoy it and stay far away from tempting toys and candy.

159. Carry a Hand Towel

Many Japanese carry small hand towels to dry their hands instead of using paper towels. I've found that these frequently come in handy for other uses.

160. Cloth Shower Curtains

VOCs are released from vinyl shower curtains, especially when they're new and heated by hot water. Several studies have linked VOCs to various forms of cancer; eye, nose, and throat irritation; headaches; nausea; and damage to the central nervous system. Cloth curtains last several times longer, can be thrown in a clothes washer, and aren't as cold when they touch your legs.

161. Cloth Diapers

Gross, I know. Disposable diapers are both environmentally damaging and much more expensive than their cloth counterparts. Modern cloth diapers don't have to be the wraps of our grandparents though; newer versions incorporate buttons or Velcro and are one size fits all. Traditional-style prefold wraps can also be made from scrap fabric, though you'll still need a diaper cover to prevent leaks. Cost comparison: 36 prefolds at $1.30 each and 18 covers of varying sizes at $6 each = $150, not including laundering cost. The average 5,625 –6,250 disposable diapers a 2 1/2 year-old has gone through at $.26 each = $1,462 - $1,625. Prefolds can also be used for burping and nursing, simplifying your diaper bag. If this really grosses you out you can buy cheap, flushable diaper liners. Cloth diapers, as odd as it sounds, also have a high resale value which means you can buy used or resale, cutting costs. Another option that deserves mention is the diaper-free movement. These caregivers stand by a no-diapers policy and rely on cues from the baby to know when it has to go. They then take the baby directly to the toilet, no diapers needed. This is a little too much effort for me, but I can see the practice's merits.

162. Homemade Baby Wipes

Mix 2 cups water, 2 tbsp baby oil or other natural oil, and 2 tbsp baby shampoo in a tall container. Cut a paper towel roll in half (brands with smaller sheets work best), remove the cardboard center, and place it inside. After the towels saturate with the mixture pull wipes from the center.

163. Breastfeeding

While we're on the topic of babies, I should mention breast feeding. A comprehensive list of breast feeding's benefits is much too vast to include here, but the most notable ones are low cost, increased closeness of mother and child, better health, stabilized temperament, less crying, a more regular sleep schedule, and little environmental impact. In terms of cost, a 6 month supply of baby formula will run anywhere from $600-$1000 and up. Compare this to $0 for exclusive breast feeding. Of course, many breastfeeding mothers use pumps and reusable bottles or supplemental formula to make their job easier. Pumps and bottles can be used for multiple children and then passed on to new mothers. Another potential benefit is that lactating women can breastfeed for a *long* time, reducing food costs well after the 6 month timeline. The World Health Organization recommends continued breast feeding for two years or more, though in the U.S. there's a bit of stigma against it.

164. Reuse Tin Foil, Sandwich Bags, Jars, and Plastic Razors.

Tin foil requires a lot of energy to produce and should be reused. Wash it off and dry completely before storing. The same goes for sandwich bags and glass jars, you'll need them to store food and medicine later. After plastic razors have dulled, run them backwards on an old strip of denim to resharpen.

165. Save Fabric

Whether it's an old T-shirt or a pair of pants, you never know when you'll need the fabric.

166. Buy Products with Less Packaging

And try to find ones in biodegradable or recyclable packaging. This won't save money, but it's a good habit to be in.

167. Newspaper Bedding for Small Animals

This may also be healthier for them as Pine and Cedar bedding damage many small animals' respiratory systems and can cause death. It once happened to a mouse we were adopting, not a happy day. Use ripped up recycled newspaper instead.

168. Old-Time Tools

I'm a big fan of old-style, human-powered tools because they require no electricity and tend to last more than one generation. The best ones are new creations that use modern technology to improve old designs. Look into modern reel mowers, apple peelers, and hand saws. If you do buy a new tool, make sure it's high quality; they don't always make them like they used to. Poke around on homesteading websites for ideas.

169. Buy Quality Shoes

I am a big fan of companies like Teva. They're overpriced just like most things, but they at least spend some proceeds on conservation projects. My first pair of Teva sandals never came apart; I only stopped wearing them after 2 1/2 years because the soles started to wear through.

170. Borrow One-time Use Items

Borrow expensive items that you will only use a few times. Examples: tuxes, suits, cameras, etc.

8 Bikes and Biodiesel

In the tips below, you'll discover how to save money on transportation in ways ranging from buying and operating a straight vegetable oil-run diesel truck for $500, to doubling your gas mileage. I've tried to keep my suggestions as pragmatic as possible, no fancy bells and whistles here, just straight forward, easy solutions. Transportation is an expensive part of most budgets, and one area you can make significant environmental improvements with easy changes. A professor once told me it would be best if everyone bought an SUV and quickly burned through all the oil on the planet. This way, he reasoned, society would have no choice but to find more environmentally-friendly methods of transportation. This is a good theory. It's also utterly wrong. Just in confirmed reserves, there is five times more oil than we can burn and still maintain a livable planet.[27] I'm not saying this as an

---

[27] If the earth warms above 2°C (3.6°F) it would be unsafe for humans. Global temperatures have already risen .8°C, and scientists estimate that producing

overzealous environmentalist; I just really like life, and want to continue liking it well into the future. With this in mind, the less pollution we produce, the better. It just so happens that the less damaging methods of transportation are also the cheapest. See the theme yet?

171. The Cheapest Cars to Drive

These are not the hybrids everyone talks about. I drive a 1994 Honda Civic hatchback that I bought in 2011 for $1000. It gets 45-54 mpg depending on the terrain. This car is 20 years old; I can only imagine what it could have done new. Cheap old cars like my Honda are easier to fix, last longer, and often get better gas millage than the vast majority of new cars. Make sure you buy something made before 1995. Shortly thereafter automakers decided their cars were lasting too long, making the consumer turnover rate slow. Good business now dictates that auto manufacturers make visually attractive vehicles that last a much shorter time.

---

another 565 gigatons of carbon dioxide will reach the two degree limit. If we instantly stopped producing CO2, temperatures would still rise another 0.8 degrees from the continuing effects of current pollution levels. Thus, we are 4/5 of the way to 2 degrees. Seriously. The Carbon Tracker Initiative out of London estimates that proven coal, oil, and gas reserves equal about 2,795 gigatons of CO2, five times the amount we can release and still maintain a 2 degree increase. Gofossilfree.org. "What Does 'Do the Math' Mean?" gofossilfree.org. http://gofossilfree.org/faq/.

172. Motor Bicycles

This is a really cool concept and even though I don't own one now, I fully intend to build one in the near future. These bicycles are mounted with a small, weed eater-sized motor that can be turned on when you get tired of pedaling. Pedal as far as you can and then ride the rest of the way. They're also highly fuel efficient; it isn't uncommon for these bicycles to get between 140-160 mpg at 40 mph, and as an added bonus, they don't require a license in most states to operate, don't require insurance, and can be made at home for less than an expensive dinner. If you don't feel comfortable fabricating one on your own (there are tutorials online and several forums with good information), you still have options; look online for companies that sell complete motor kits, buy a completed bike locally (craigslist is a good place to look), or ask around to find someone who can build it for you.

173. Body Modifications

This one is a lot of fun. Remember that Honda Civic I drive? It's a well-designed car, meant to be a gas saver. It's streamlined and low to the ground, just the way an intelligently-designed car should be. My Honda averages 48 mpg without body modifications, but there are stories floating around of modified Civics which get over 90! If this is a little too fantastic for you, there are several well-documented modified Civics that get around 70 mpg. Although the exact body alterations vary depending on the type of car you drive, a few basics apply across the board. Attaching fins to the car's sides and nose, lowering them to ground level, and extending your roof (on hatchbacks) further back with a slight downward slope to reduce drag are the most effective options. Look online for more information and designs for your particular vehicle. There is a large community of hypermilers out there who love to share their achievements and have already done the difficult design work for you.

174. Vegetable Oil Diesel

Again, this doesn't have to be expensive, although companies trying to capitalize on the market would lead you to believe so. My friend Kurt owns an old 2-tank diesel truck. You can buy one on craigslist for $500. He fills one tank with regular diesel and the other with strained kitchen grease from restaurants in town. Once every few weeks, he drives into town and fills his tank, for free. The easiest way to get access to grease is to talk with local restaurant owners; they'll likely be fascinated by what you're doing and willing to help. To operate the truck, all you have to do is start it with regular diesel, and after it warms up, switch over to the bio tank. When you're done driving around, switch back to diesel and give it time to run through the fuel lines. In a truck that would normally get 12 miles per gallon of diesel, Kurt gets over 100.

175. Learn to Drive

Knowing how to drive well goes beyond simply knowing the law and getting from point A to point B. Learn to drive a manual transmission – it gives you the control needed to be a skillful gas-saving driver. I learned how to drive a manual after I bought one and drove it over an hour back home, stalling multiple times at each red light along the way. I could drive fairly well within a week. Drive slow, less than 55 mph. You lose 3% efficiency at 60 mph, 8% at 65, 17% at 70, 23% at 75, and 28% at 80. This is why the U.S. government instituted a nation-wide ban on speed limits over 55 mph after the 1973 oil crisis; driving at 55 mph saves a significant amount of fuel (and money). Other ways to drive efficiently include accelerating slowly and coasting to stops, especially red lights, and trying to avoid complete stops all together. It takes more fuel to move a stationary car than one already in motion. You can also plan your route ahead of time to maximize right turns. This is the same technique FedEx and UPS uses to reduce expenses.

Remember that hills can be your friends, and coast in neutral (only with a manual transmission) whenever possible. If you'll be idling longer than 30 seconds, turn your car off. See www.fueleconomy.gov, www.mpgforspeed.com, or Natural Resources Canada (remember this will be in kph) for more information.

176. Additional Gas-saving Tips

1) Take out any extra weight you can find. 2) Keep your vehicle tuned up. 3) Change oil and air filters, keep track of oil changes, and make sure you have good oxygen sensors. 4) Check your tire pressure frequently and refill if necessary.[28] Underinflated tires can hamper your fuel mileage by 4-10%. 5) Buy tires with less rolling resistance.

177. Trucks and SUVs

Unless you need it, really *need* it, don't drive a truck or SUV. If you live on a farm or are in the construction business a truck is great to own, but don't drive it around town. Most of us think we need an SUV, but we really don't. Except in the

---

[28] You can use a bike pump to inflate small amounts, though it will take a fair amount of effort.

case of biodiesel, trucks and SUVs consume too much gas to fit into a no-work lifestyle. Go online to www.fueleconomy.gov/feg/savemoney.shtml and plug in your current vehicle's MPG and that of a more fuel-efficient vehicle. The calculator will tell you how much more expensive the first vehicle will be to run over the course of a year. Take this amount and divide it by your hourly wage to see just how many hours you have to work keep your vehicle.[29]

178. Buy From Car Auctions

Sometimes you can find great deals at car auctions. The online listings show the exact cars to be sold, just make sure the auction isn't for dealers only.

179. Don't Fill Your Gas Tank

At least not all the way. Gas needs room to expand or it will be expelled unburnt out of your exhaust.

---

[29] If you are on salary this still applies. Take your net yearly salary minus yearly work-related expenses and divide it by the number of weeks you work. Then further divide it by the total number of hours you typically work each week *plus* how many hours you spend on work-related activities each week (look at tip 224 for a more detailed explanation of how to calculate your relative income). Thus, a person who earns $35,000/yr after taxes, spends $5,000/yr on work-related expenses, and works a total of 50 weeks (subtracting the typical 2 weeks of vacation) makes $600/wk. Assuming they work an average of 40 hours each week and spend an additional 9 hours on work-related activities (getting ready, commuting, winding down after work, etc.), they end up making $12.25/hr.

180. Use Public Transportation

No more finding parking spaces or paying for vehicle upkeep and gas. You can use the commute to read, think, or do something productive.

181. Bike

If you live close enough.

182. Walk

Just like biking and public transport, walking gives you time to think and sort out your thoughts. This is something we as a society have nearly lost. Think about it, what do you do when you walk? You think. What about when you drive? I listen to music. Walking also keeps you fit.

183. Carpool

First, find out if there are any carpools in your neighborhood. If not, talk to your neighbors or put up fliers to start one. There are also online rideshare communities you can join that work like social networking sites; you create a profile with a few bits of information about yourself and use the site to find or create carpools. Zimride.com is a good one. Carpooling may also give you access to special lane or parking privileges.

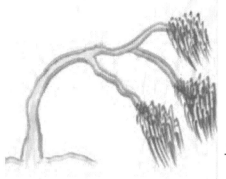

9 Better Design, Better Life

The building you live in has a direct impact on how easy or difficult it is to live without a job. Although most people don't think of it this way, in numerous ways a house actually defines your lifestyle. So the question that follows, is how to alter the building's design to match the easy life. I'll introduce some considerations in this chapter.

In the following tips, I explain the basics of cheap, highly energy-efficient building design and modifications, a little sustainable building philosophy, and my favorite, <u>how your house can make you money on a regular basis</u>. I also introduce several larger topics, such as earthship design and micro hydroelectric power, that need much more space to fully explain than I have here. You can find more information on each of these online, complete with DIY guides and support communities. When you build your home, build it to fit your worldview and interests. If you like outdoor spaces and trapeze arts, don't build a 4-walled box with low ceilings. In terms of worldview, simple design features influence, and at least partially determine, how you see the world. The street light out back says the dark is scary; walls subconsciously separate you from everything outside, assisting in the misapprehension that we are somehow intrinsically different than everything else; and the straight, rigid lines of conventional houses separate us psychologically from the fluid and mixing reality of nature. Keep this in mind, and remember that even if you are unaware of it, your home helps create who you are.

    This is not an exhaustive list of alternative construction methods; it's a list of introductions that I hope will open other doors for you and your design. Of course, remember that construction is environmentally damaging and the more sustainable option in most cases is to modify your existing home rather than build new.

184. Permaculture

Permaculture is a philosophy of building, gardening, and living designed to bring humans closer to the natural world and environmentally-ethical living. It's centered on three core concepts: First, take care of the earth. Second, take care of people. Third, set limits to consumption and reproduction while redistributing surplus. If you're interested in ecological housing design, this is a good place to start as permaculture is more of an umbrella term that encompasses diverse environmental design principles, most of which are not included in this book. Permaculture mimics natural processes and in doing so eliminates all waste, saves energy, and saves you a lot of work. You can find more information at www.permaculture.org or, even better, videos of an entire course on permaculture from NC State University are available at www.courses.ncsu.edu/hs432/common/podcasts.

185. Alternative Building Materials and Modified Structures

People have made homes from a variety of unexpected things. Old grain silos and underground missile bunkers are good examples. Think outside the four-walled box house and see what you can come up with. Pieces of large culvert piping make excellent hallways (when properly insulated and waterproofed), and recycled material from abandoned industrial sites (that you have legal access to) provide industrial-strength structural supports. Your local building codes may not allow the use of certain materials. Remember that you can use them for non-residential structures as well. It's hard to envision, but these recycled structures can be made beautiful with a good surface treatment and a little ingenuity. On the natural materials side, mud-straw construction is a good option. It's environmentally-friendly, cheap, and well-suited for dry climates. You can find more information on mud-straw construction at www.strawbale.com. Cordwood construction is also energy-efficient and cost-effective. As an added plus, it's easy to learn and quick to build with. Earth bags are yet another eco-option that are easy to use and provide high thermal mass. Remember that these alternative techniques and materials can be used on non-residential structures as well.

186. Modify the Design, Not the Environment

There are roads in the jungles of Columbia built over 1,000 years ago that are still standing and usable. There are roads in the U.S. built two decades ago that are filled with potholes. Why is this? One reason is that the people who built the Columbian roads built *with* the land rather than altering the land to match their designs. Look at virtually any ancient structure and you'll see how well building in tune with the surrounding area works. This isn't a new concept. Altering the environment to match pre-established, mass-produced designs is the new concept. To translate this into your design, look at your plot of land first, and then design your home to fit it. This way you can capitalize on the land's strengths and decrease the amount of work needed to build on it.

187. Know What a Home Is

A house is not separate from the rest of the environment; once built, it's part of it. To encourage peaceful feelings and mutually-beneficial interactions with local plant and animal life, your house should become both an appropriate, and a productive, part of the environment.

188. Build Small and Comfortable

More size equals more of everything else; more cleaning, more upkeep, and more expense. The smaller you build, the easier the house will be to take care of. Of course, you don't want to build something that will be too small should unexpected children (or grandchildren) arrive.

189. Make Your Home Support You

Both your house and the surrounding environment should work together for their mutual benefit. Some ways to support the surrounding environment are to build green space, irrigation systems, and/or animal habitats into your house. In the other direction, let water/wind/solar power, garden space, and natural beauty support you. It's possible to build a home that powers itself, accentuates the natural beauty of the area, and grows its own food.

190. Know Your Microclimate

Microclimates can make or break your dream home and should be considered even when renting or buying a house. The climate of a particular area, even one as small as a few feet, can drastically differ from nearby spaces. For example, when I was young we had a lot of snow during the winter. I learned early on that in some nooks of the mountains snow would remain unbroken until late spring, long after it had melted everywhere else. One of these locations was also the best place to get icicles over 6 feet long. As you can probably guess, this was also the coolest area during summer. Anyone looking at the property in the summertime would have found the cool temperatures quite appealing. But come winter, they would have frozen for months.

There are several things to consider when looking at your microclimate: 1) Water and/or urban areas can have cooling/heating effects. Urban areas hold heat, running water keeps things cool, and large bodies of standing water mitigate temperature fluctuations.[30] 2) Wind patterns

---

[30] Because of its high thermal mass.

caused by topography or the lack of vegetation can create gentle breezes or fierce gusts. 3) Topography can make other uncommon weather patterns common. 4) The amount of sunlight the area receives will have a significant impact on temperature and brightness. 5) Too much humidity combined with poor circulation can make for mold-ridden homes. 6) Air circulation impacts air quality, pollution levels, and mold growth. 7) Plant cover serves various functions, including temperature regulation and noise pollution control. 8) The thermal mass of your soil type impacts heat gain and loss.

191. Build in a Thermal Belt

It's rational to assume that the further down a mountain you go, the warmer it will be. After all, the higher you climb the cooler it seems to get, right? Although normally true, this is not always the case. Certain combinations of hills and valleys can create thermal belts on the side of slopes, a phenomenon wherein cool nighttime air flows into the valley pushing up the warm air trapped there.[31] This warm air creates a thermal belt usually 200-300 meters above the valley floor. Above this belt, air begins to

---

[31] This normally happens when there is a city in the valley creating a heat island.

cool rapidly. My first experience with thermal belts was in my second apartment. My apartment was about three miles from my university, uphill, and above the main city. Every winter night I was bewildered when it would be cold at school while at my apartment, less than three miles away, it was several degrees warmer. As it turns out, I lived in a sweet spot on the mountain. This made a huge difference in personal comfort and winter heating. For more information on thermal belts and various other microclimate factors look around on www.permaculture.org.

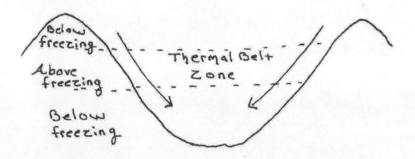

192. Earth-sheltered Housing

Underground or earth-bermed housing is the way to go in Appalachia and a good option in most other areas not prone to flooding. In a nutshell, what you need to know about earth-sheltered construction is that you can, and many people do, build homes either completely underground or bermed with earth. Think of Bilbo Baggins' home and you'll have an idea of what earth-sheltered housing looks like. There's a reason this is the oldest construction technique still used around the world – it's safe, cheap, and maintains a relatively constant, comfortable internal temperature. Earth-sheltered houses also tend to be healthier, require less upkeep, and offer increased potential for sustainable living over conventional construction. If this hasn't convinced you, imagine telling people you have a garden on your roof. Super cool.

Completely underground houses are resistant to natural disasters. Because they are underground, tornados pose less of a threat and earthquakes can't topple them. The threat of fire is also reduced because underground houses are usually constructed primarily out of fire-proof materials, like concrete, and are surrounded by dirt. They do, however, have to be properly waterproofed and located in an area with good drainage. Mudslides are not a good thing either, so if you build in a hillside make sure there is plenty of vegetation up the hill to hold the soil down. There are various construction techniques and materials for earth-sheltered homes, and the cost of building a new one can vary dramatically depending on the technique used. At the high end, you can hire companies who specialize in earth-sheltered houses and build them using conventional methods. At the cheap end, you can use earth packed in small bags, called earth bags, which are inexpensive (though labor intensive to make), and avoid the harmful off-gassing that accompanies new construction.

With 6 inches of earth cover, an underground house will maintain a year-round internal temperature between 50-60 degrees and will never drop below 50-55. This means that if the walls are well insulated,[32] heating the inside of the home requires less energy because the difference between the desired internal temperature and the actual external temperature is less significant. Combine this with the high thermal mass of building materials, passive solar, and a grey water heat conservation system, and you have free heat in a home that requires no air conditioning.

It took me a while to realize this, but there's a big difference between insulation and thermal mass; they both regulate heat but do so in very

---

[32] Although the specifics of how to properly insulate an earth-sheltered home lie outside the scope of this book, I want to explain that underground homes should be covered with a waterproofing membrane and then insulated on the *outside* of the waterproofing. This ensures that temperature fluctuations do not cause the inside of the waterproofing membrane to sweat. Many books on the subject fail to mention this necessary detail.

different ways. Thermal mass mitigates temperature change but doesn't hold heat inside. In fact, a high mass object transfers heat from warm areas to cool ones, meaning that in an uninsulated underground house the walls and floor will wick heat away from the interior. Insulation does the opposite; the better the insulation, the worse it is at transferring heat. This is why insulation holds back both heat and cold. Lastly, with underground houses you don't have to replace siding or roofing, though depending on your design you may have to mow it. Odd idea, isn't it?

193. So...Isn't it Dark Underground?

Underground houses are not dark caves like most people think they are. They can be easily well-lit with natural light, a source proven to make inhabitants feel better than artificial lighting. Skylights and sun tubes are popular choices because they don't require energy.

194. Earthships

An Earthship is a sustainable home built using recycled materials and rammed earth, combining high thermal mass, low-cost, and environmental consciousness. It's really more of a philosophy of building than it is a method. The most popular technique is to stack used tires as you would bricks and ram them full of earth. Tires can be gathered for free from many mechanic shops. Waterproof the outside and plaster the inside of the structure and you have a nice, artistic home. Done well, visitors will have no idea your walls are made of tires; the wave pattern looks intentional (and expensive). If you're building above ground, use a mixture of cob[33] and earthen plasters for both the inside and outside walls.

195. Microhydro

If you have moving water on your property, chances are you can either eliminate or significantly reduce your electric bill by creating your own energy. Microhydro power is hydroelectric power built on a small scale, often only 1-2 houses per power unit. In the past, water power centered on a revolutionary but antiquated invention: the waterwheel. Waterwheels are attractive and can be modified to produce more than enough power for a household, but microhydro water turbines produce more power with less water and less space. There are multiple ways to implement microhydro: If there is enough fall from water source to turbine, water can be piped into it. If there isn't enough fall but you can build a small waterfall, 1 ft.

---

[33] A mixture of clay and straw. For more information visit www.strawbale.com.

high or so, you can install a turbine designed for this. Finally, if neither of these options work, there are long turbines that are designed to span small streams.

196. Waterwheels

If you don't want to buy a turbine (they're difficult to make, though I've only been privy to one construction attempt), the best homemade hydroelectric power option is the waterwheel. There is a gentleman in my neck of the woods who runs three full-sized houses with the energy his single, 18 ft. diameter waterwheel produces. He claims that a 1/2 inch stream of water can run his wheel. I believe it. This thing is so heavy that once you get it moving, even without water weight, I can't stop it. There are three primary types of waterwheels; the undershot wheel, breast wheel, and overshot wheel. Research different ways the energy output of the wheel can be amplified.

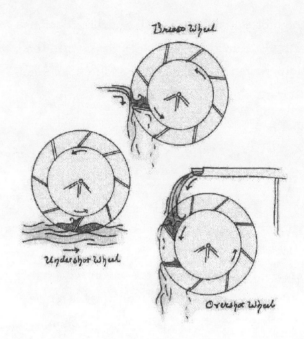

197. Other Sources of Alternative Energy

Because hydropower works so well where I live, I don't know much about how to implement other alternative energy sources. The major options are wind, solar, wave, and geothermal power. Whichever solution you decide to go with, first look up your state's laws as they determine how energy can be produced and how it can be used. For example, in many areas self-produced energy can be directed into the electric grid where it becomes part of the pool everyone can access. This 'Grid-Tied' system has pros and cons. One of the major cons is that copper electrical wire loses energy through friction. The further the energy travels, the more it magically disappears. On the positive side, as you pump energy into the grid your meter will run backwards. If you don't use as much energy as you produce, the power company may *pay you* for those leftover kilowatts. Whether they buy your energy or simply give you energy credits is determined by the company itself. This way, if you produce enough energy, your house can literally provide checks on an annual basis.

198. Build Your Own Wind Turbines and Solar Panels

Check out tutorials on these and other DIY options on www.instructables.com.

199. Energy-efficient Modifications for Free

Federal and state rebates, along with other financial incentives, will pay part or all of many energy-efficient home improvements. Some utility companies offer rebates on low-flow showerheads and fixtures. Other green improvements, such as adding insulation or painting your roof white, may come with tax credits or other incentives. My local power board even offers free energy audits and lists over a hundred money-saving suggestions on their website. See what yours offers. Look around on www.energystar.gov and www.dsireusa.org for the opportunities that apply to you.

200. Plant Trees

Deciduous trees on the sunny south side of a house block summer sun while allowing it through during winter. Evergreens to the north cut down on wind chill heat loss and provide summer shade. As an added bonus, planting trees keeps the area partially wooded, allowing small animals to inhabit it and helping mitigate some of the damage caused by new construction.

201. Trees Make You Happier

They really do. Several research studies have shown that people tend to feel happier when they're surrounded by greenery.

202. Food-bearing Trees

If you're going to plant trees anyway, it makes sense to choose some that produce nuts or fruit. You can eat the food, store it, or let neighbors come collect their fill.

203. Select Appropriate Native Varieties

Part of living in harmony with your local environment is to help it stay local. Exotic plants can upset an ecosystem's balance. Also, select trees that will grow to match your intentions; some varieties grow faster, are taller, wider, and have deeper roots than others.

204. Building Orientation

I mentioned this in the energy chapter but will briefly revisit it. Direct windows and as much wall space as possible to the south to maximize wintertime solar heat gain.

205. Heater Options

Two comfortable homesteading heater options are corn burners and wood stoves. Select designs that are efficient and pollute less than conventional ones. My friend Rod has one of the best designs I've seen; it's built out of brick, relying on its thermal mass, and recycles and burns unburnt fumes.[34] When using a radiant heat source like a wood stove or passive solar design, be sure to incorporate thermal mass to capture and store the heat. If you leave this part out, your home will heat up and cool

---

[34] Look online for DIY designs. Motherearthnews.com is a good place to start.

down too quickly. If you decide to design your own heater, follow these basic heating principles:
1) Heat rises. 2) Incorporate thermal mass.
3) A glazed surface is necessary for solar heat.
4) Radiant heat is more comfortable than forced air.
5) Fuel is easy to use but requires effort to procure while sunlight does not. 6) Air must be replaced in order to move. The smaller the space, the less air is able to move within it. This is why fluffy insulation works so well; the air pockets inside are too small for the heat to cause convection.[35]

206. Passive Solar Systems

The cheapest and most eco-friendly heaters rely on the sun. Trombe walls, greenhouse walls connected to the outside of your house's south-facing side, solar heat grabbers, and completely external greenhouses that collect and pipe in heat are the best options. All of these systems work the same basic way: by capturing solar radiation, storing it, and circulating it inside. In external greenhouses, this effect can be created by placing plants on boards spanning several black plastic barrels of water. As sunlight strikes the barrels it's absorbed, providing free heat while accelerating the

---

[35] This is the same phenomenon you experience in the shower when the curtain touches your legs. Air heated by the water rises up and over the curtain where it rapidly cools and falls. This motion pulls in new air from under the curtain, creating a cycle.

plants' growth. Vent pipes connecting the greenhouse to the main house can be opened at will, allowing heat to flow in. The other options, Trombe walls, connected greenhouses, and solar heat grabbers, are all very similar.

For existing houses, the solar hear grabber is a good choice; it's cheap and easy to make. This unit captures heat in an insulated box and pushes it into your home by simultaneously pulling out cooler air. That air is then heated and the cycle repeats itself. On a sunny day, the grabber will generate thousands of BTU's of heat. More information and designs for the solar heat grabber as well as the other options I've mentioned can be found at www.motherearthnews.com and www.builditsolar.com.

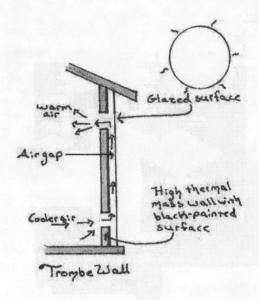

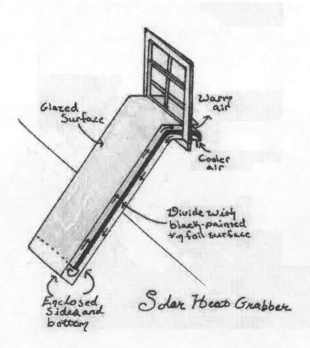

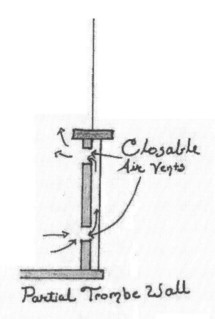

Partial Trombe Wall

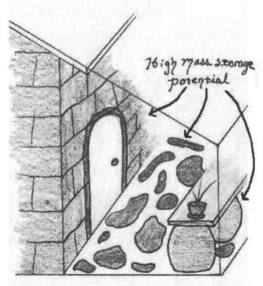

Greenhouse Wall

207. Earthen Paint

It's possible, and rather easy and inexpensive, to make your own paint. There are three parts to paint: pigment, binder, and filler. Each does what its name suggests. Colors can be created from various plant and soil/mineral sources. Starch found in flour, casein found in milk, and linseed oil can be used as binders to hold the mix together. Common fillers that add bulk, but that can also add unique textures, include whiting (powered chalk), talcum, limestone, and clay. Earthen paints are not just limited to earth tones. Bright, vibrant colors can also be produced. Visit www.earthpigments.com for more information.

208. Earthen Floors

High clay-content earth can also be used to make attractive, durable, and super cheap flooring. Sealed earthen floors are dirt-free (on top of course) and can be mopped and swept. They can also be customized by adding texture, color, tiles, and mosaics. When insulated well, earthen floors also have excellent passive heating potential. Search 'earthen floors' on www.motherearthliving.com for more information and how-to guides from people who've installed them.

209. Rain Collection

Collecting rain water is an easy way to reduce environmental impact and water bills. The simplest way to do this is to catch rain gutter runoff in a barrel. I suggest using the water for your garden or house plants rather than cleaner in-home uses; it can get kinda scummy if you leave it outside too long.

210. Use Good Windows

Choose double and triple-paned windows with high R-values. These windows reduce heat transfer by sandwiching a small sealed airspace between the panes. Choose glazed windows if you need to reflect heat without losing light. When you can, buy windows from bargain salvage yards or collect ones that have been discarded during remodels; they are often too expensive to purchase at full price. During my junior year of college, all the windows in my apartment complex were replaced. It was a big complex. Although they were old, most were in perfectly good shape; the owner simply wanted to save on labor costs by replacing all the windows at once. I asked one of the workers, and he was more than happy to let me take as many as I wanted. He had already taken four himself. Forty of these wood-framed windows found their way into my apartment, and then into our barn. We used five in my grandfather's new log cabin less than a year later.

211. Tankless and Operable Water Heaters

Because large tank heaters run constantly, they are the second largest energy consumer in American homes, accounting for 18% of the average energy bill.[36] Tankless heaters, also called on-demand heaters, are more expensive up front but save money in the long term by only heating water as it's needed. The more people you have in your household, the more cost effective these heaters are. For smaller families, a better option is an easy-to-install small tank heater. These 1-6 gallon tanks can be turned on and off as needed; just switch it on and let it heat up before you shower. Both of these heaters can be found in electric and gas varieties. I suggest buying a cheap option to use as a supplement to your even cheaper solar water heater.

---

[36] Energy.gov. "Tips: Water Heating". Energy.gov. May 2, 2012. http://energy.gov/energysaver/articles/tips-water-heating. This percentage will be much higher after you reduce or eliminate your heating and cooling costs.

10 Finances

Some of the most effective ways to save money involve money itself. When possible, it's better to make your money work for you rather than the other way around. Want free airline tickets and weddings? What about permanently reducing your property taxes and making money on environmentally-friendly businesses? It's all here. This section also deals with the environmental impacts of our financial decisions. Most of us wouldn't intentionally invest our money in businesses that then use it to profit from deforestation, mass pollution, and mountaintop removal, a practice where entire mountain tops, like those in Kentucky and West Virginia, are literally blown off to look for coal. But the unfortunate reality is that almost all of us do invest in these businesses, albeit unintentionally. Credit card companies, banks, and insurance companies all invest the money you give them into these environmentally-destructive industries. Why? These investments tend to have the highest returns. Our bank, credit card, and insurance companies would never make a point to mention this, and none of their customers would know without looking into the company's investments themselves. Fortunately, there are more environmentally-friendly alternatives.

212. Socially Responsible Investing (SRI)

Instead of donating to causes you love, invest in them. Donations, when given to the right cause, can be great agents of social good. However, they are, by their nature, a one-time deal and organizations who rely on them often cannot function without support from their donors. This, I'm afraid, isn't very sustainable.[37] Instead of trying to influence a problem from the outside, a more sustainable (and I believe effective) alternative is to change the cause of the problem itself. In most cases, this means changing business. How do you change business? Become a shareholder with a voice. The idea is simple; businesses that are supported do well while businesses that aren't don't. If investors make it known that environmental consciousness, for example, is important to them and their investment

---

[37] Although for some causes monetary donations may be the only viable option. However, for other causes, such as animal rights, environmental protection, and workers' rights, a more effective solution is to invest as I explain here.

decisions, businesses have no choice but to adopt more environmentally-conscious practices. It's just good business. All we have to do is make that push. Luckily, there are already thousands of investors who are and they've made the process incredibly easy for the rest of us.

Now for the technical details. If you have particular companies in mind and the time to watch their performance and business decisions, you can invest in individual stocks. Or, if you're like me and would rather use those hours to play racquetball or do something else more important, you can invest in Socially Responsible mutual funds instead. SRI mutual funds are organized around ethical principles. In other words, they invest in companies that match their ethical criteria while still striving to make money for you, the investor. By investing in socially responsible mutual funds, you support companies with ethical guidelines similar to your own, encourage others to improve their business practices, and, if you stay in the market long enough, potentially make money. Activism that pays. Nice. I'm a personal fan of funds focusing on alternative energy and animal rights. PAX World funds are good choices and have a low, $250 initial investment minimum. With PAX World, you can invest in animal rights, human/workers' rights, environmental rights, and women's rights along with several others.

When shopping around for a mutual fund, look into the actual investments within the fund. Many fund managers take a lazy approach to their job, and so their 'Socially Responsible' funds pay a lot of lip service, but not a lot of attention to the companies they invest in. Look at the top 5 companies a fund invests in and ask yourself, 'Why it this company included?' For example, some fund managers only invest in companies that have a positive environmental record, while other fund managers invest in large companies with poor environmental records in order to use the fund's influence to encourage better practices. Both approaches are effective, but many fund managers know, and plan on the fact, that even if big companies don't change, they still provide big returns. Lastly, the size of the mutual fund partially determines how much influence it will have on corporations.

In my experience, going with a self-directed broker like Scottrade is easier and more likely to ensure your ethical objectives are met than hiring a traditional broker to help guide your portfolio. When I started investing, I met with several brokers trying to find one who could help direct my investments. It soon became obvious that each of them were interested in one thing only: manipulating investments to make money. Of course, this makes sense because it's most of their job. However, none of them understood my environmental/social objectives or seemed to know how to act on them. I decided to invest by myself and I'm glad I did. Investing in any form is a fairly complex subject so you should research everything thoroughly. To get started, order the free mutual fund guide from www.socialfunds.com.

213. Another Alternative to Donating to Charity

That sounds really bad, doesn't it? I'm not against donating to charity, but if there's a way of furthering your cause while simultaneously increasing your potential of doing so again in the future, I think that is the more intelligent and sustainable option.[38] Instead of giving your money away, consider giving a no-interest loan. Through www.energyincommon.org you can give low-income families around the world loans for sustainable development and clean energy. If development will continue either way, it might as well have solar panels on its roof. After the family repays the loan, you can make another one and continue to make positive changes in the world.

---

[38] Though I also believe that donations, when given with a selfless attitude and a thorough analysis of their outcomes, are a wonderful way of improving the lives of others and your own sense of self.

214. Conservation Easements

Conservation easements are a little-known way to reduce property taxes while simultaneously permanently conserving private land. A conservation easement is a legal agreement between the land owner and a land trust or government agency that restricts the development potential of a piece of land. The original owner continues to own the land and can will it, sell it, or give it away as normal, but the land will be permanently bound by the easement. My neighbors Peter and Jane first introduced me to this concept. They own a lot of land, somewhere around 200 acres, that they bought in the mountains of Western North Carolina during the late 1970's. They're homesteaders in the most traditional sense of the word, and have a deep appreciation for the natural beauty of the mountains. It's understandable then, that as they watched the surrounding forestland they love so much being developed at an increasing pace, they sought out ways to protect what they could. They soon discovered that if they put a conservation easement on their land, and donated that easement to a conservation land trust, they could not only protect the land after their deaths, but that the easement also qualified them for a tax deduction (that they didn't need), would reduce the estate tax when they will the land to their children, and reduced their property taxes.

According to their agreement (individual terms are somewhat flexible), Peter and Jane retain full ownership of the land and can build three more structures at any point in the future in addition to the house, barn, and canning shed they've already built. Once a year, a representative of the land trust visits and does a survey of the property to make sure the agreement is being followed. This usually happens in the following way: The representative (who Peter and Jane know by name), comes over for lunch. After they've eaten their fill, the three walk around to look at that year's crop and survey the property. After shooting the breeze for a couple of hours and another cup of mint tea, the three say goodbye until next year. Peter, who as you might guess knows a lot more about this than I do, says that land trusts are most interested in property that is either large, mostly undeveloped, or that borders another easement, National Park, or National Forest.

215. Maximize Income Tax Deductions

Charitable donations, certain green home improvements, and traditional IRA deposits (does not include ROTH IRAs) are among many tax deductible options. If you make enough money to benefit from tax deductions, look into as many options as you can.

216. Have Your Property Reassessed

If you think you're paying too much in property tax, having your property reassessed may lower it.

217. Buy Catastrophic Medical Insurance

Catastrophic medical insurance is the cheapest non-subsidized option. Buy one with the highest deductible you're positive you can afford; this usually means lower monthly payments. You either know (or will soon know) how to treat minor illnesses and injuries yourself, but there's always the potential of a major medical emergency. If this happens, you don't want to be caught without insurance. If you still don't want to carry insurance, you'll be penalized under the new healthcare law.

See if you qualify for an exemption; most people living the work-free life do: www.healthcare.gov/exemptions.

218. Life Insurance

Your basic options are term life, whole life, and return of premium. Term life lasts for a set number of years, after which rates will increase if you want to renew the policy. Whole life requires higher monthly payments but doesn't expire. Return of premium is a term policy wherein if you don't die before your policy is up, you get all your money back. This sounds great, doesn't it? It isn't a bad option, but if you're pretty sure you will outlive the term, a better option is probably to forgo the insurance policy altogether and invest a standard amount each month into stock options (see tip on Socially Responsible Investing). Set this 'savings' account aside, and if you live to an old age, there should be plenty there to play with.

The reason investing the money yourself may be a better option than return of premium is that $5,000 today is not the same as $5,000 in 20 years. When you get your premium back in a lump sum, the purchasing value of that sum will be much less than when you first handed it over. Investing directly is a way to keep up with inflation and most likely add a little on top.[39] Of course, instead of trying to secure more money for death, you could reduce the cost of death and thus alleviate the need for so much money. This will cause fewer headaches as well. Look into environmentally-friendly burial options (not the ones offered by profit-motivated companies); they tend to cost less.

219. Increase Auto Insurance Deductible

Most people who live the work-free life don't have more than liability coverage, but if you do, increase your deductible. This should lower your monthly payments.

220. If Other People Will Pay You to do Things, Let Them

It isn't difficult to get corporate and private sponsors for anything from travel to weddings. If you're part of an organization that is well-known or just sounds official, call local businesses and ask for donations. If not, go in person (and in nice clothes) and ask the manager if s/he is willing to sponsor your activity in

---

[39] Although mutual funds are less volatile than individual stocks, any investment may not pan out well. Invest at your own risk.

exchange for advertising. Be straightforward and tell him/her what the donation is for. Be polite, professional, and specific about what you want. Ask a lot of businesses. In my experience, getting donations is actually quite easy, especially when you ask for gift cards. I've heard of entire weddings thrown for free and personally know that some wedding professionals will offer discounts if you promise there will be other couples present who may hire down the road. Framed in this way, your event becomes less a job and more of an advertising opportunity. The key here is to find out what the person wants and offer it to them in exchange for lower-priced/free stuff and services.

221. *Travel Credit Cards*

If you are a frequent traveler, consider getting a reward-producing credit card. For each dollar you spend you'll earn a set number of miles which can then be used to purchase plane tickets. Several cards also have signup bonuses ranging from 5,000-10,000 miles if you spend a certain amount in the first few months. Pick one with no foreign transaction fees. These are credit cards so I suggest only charging the amount you can pay off before the grace period ends. After this time, balances begin accruing interest and can get out of hand. Credit cards don't magically produce free plane tickets, and one 'mile' in your account doesn't equal one linear mile of travel, but if you're spending money either way there's no reason not to use one.

222. Sustainable Airlines

When flying, consider using airlines that actively work towards greener travel. The top eco-airlines are:

Best American Airlines
Virgin America: Virgin has been ranked the most environmentally-friendly airline four years in a row by Greenopia based on fuel conservation practices, progress on alternative fuel, green food choices, recycling projects, and carbon offsets. Other high rankers are Alaska, United, Jet Blue, and Delta.

Best European Airlines:
Air France, Lufthansa, British Airways, Virgin Atlantic, and Easy Jet.

223. Eco-friendly Credit Cards

Large credit card companies exist for one reason: to make money. Unfortunately, some of the biggest moneymaking industries out there involve logging, coal, and petroleum. To keep from inadvertently funding causes you disagree with, try green credit cards. The Working Assets Visa Signature card and Salmon Nation Visa Card are among the best. Working Assets donates a flat $.10 to a nonprofit of your choice for each purchase you make while Shorebank, the lender behind Salmon Nation card, donates half of the card's profits to protect Pacific salmon habitats.

224. *Think of Money as Time*

Too often we think of money as money. If you work at a job that requires a time commitment, money isn't money, it's time. Thinking of money as the amount of time you spend getting it will give you a better understanding of what you're trading for each purchase. There are two steps to this process. First, calculate your relative income, that is, how much money you actually make each hour.[40] This isn't the same as your hourly wage. Think of all the money you spend directly related to earning money: gas used getting to work and back, car maintenance, and all the meals you eat out for lunch instead of bringing your own. Add up these expenses to determine how much you spend each week just to be able to work. Subtract that number from the amount you earn each week after taxes, and divide the remainder by the total number of hours you spend each week on work-related

---

[40] Again, if you are on salary this still applies. See note #29.

activities. This includes not only time at work, but also time spent on your commute, morning preparation, email outside of work time, and even winding down after work in front of the TV. Add everything up. The equation looks like this: (Weekly net earnings − weekly work expenses) / total time required for work = your real hourly wage. The amount may surprise you.

The second step is to think of purchases in terms of how much time they cost. For example, a $500 TV, when you're really only earning $7.50 an hour, costs over a week and a half of full time labor. Thinking of money in this way can actually help you loosen up a bit as well. I have a bad habit of being too frugal, and sometimes miss out on experiences because of their expense. Realizing how much time certain luxuries cost has actually helped me loosen up and spend more, though I still find $5 coffees at Starbucks hard to swallow.

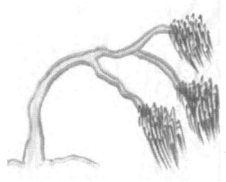

11 Play, Travel, and Community

Part of the fun of living in the middle is increasing the amount of time you have to play and building a stronger community around you. It's also pretty cool to have enough time to travel and explore the world. How will you travel with no money you ask? Truthfully, you need some money, but traveling doesn't have to be nearly as expensive as most people make it. Normally, as long as you can get there (and there are super cheap ways of doing this too, like $300 round-trip from New York to London cheap[41]), you can get free housing, free tour guides, and oftentimes, free food in almost any country in the world. If you happen to land in an area where English instruction is in high demand, particularly East Asia, it's easy to trade a few hours of conversation time for money, stay, or food. I was once even able to trade two hours of SAT test prep every Friday for half price rent in a nice house. We had a servant, marble floors, and leather furniture. Total price tag for

---

[41] I'm experimenting with this now and plan to include more information in the second edition of this book.

a private room including meals...$90 USD/month.[42] I learned that wealthy parents want their kids to study in America, and because you're either from America or can speak English, you can help them get there. They'll pay you well for it.

As far as community goes, a strong community supports itself and makes living without a job immensely easier than going at it alone. Friends will be there to help out when you need them, there will be free garden produce abound, and you will have plenty of reasons to get out of bed and do things when there are others to do them with. It's a mutually beneficial relationship, and you should never hesitate to help a neighbor without good reason. Your community doesn't end with your human neighbors though; it also includes the animal and plant life around you. This wide definition helps ensure you look out for your larger community, an investment that will pay off in the future not only for you, but also for those who come after.

---

[42] This isn't as obnoxious as it sounds. The young man who was our servant (and friend) was from a poor family in an area with no jobs, by giving him a job (and it was a fairly relaxed one) we were able to substantially improve his quality of life. Not having to do my own laundry was just a bonus.

225. Free Housing (almost) Anywhere in the World

It's easy to get. For short-term stays, check out www.globalfreeloaders.com and www.couchsurfing.org. These are online communities of people who enjoy meeting new faces, having new experiences, and will offer you a free place to sleep. Using these online databases, you can find new friends to stay with in over 200 countries. In return, it's expected that you offer a 'couch' for travelers in your area when you can. Both systems are based on give and take; they can't function otherwise. Almost always the host will be willing to show you around, letting you see a side of the area you wouldn't otherwise get to. Both communities have an excellent reputation. For long-term housing, check out www.homeexchange.com. This is a home exchange listing that covers more than 85 countries. There's a small membership fee on this site.

226. Finding New Friends Abroad, Free City Tours, and More Free Housing

Hospitalityclub.org is an online community of people who want to meet foreigners and show them around. Sometimes they'll offer free housing as well.

Currently, there are over 200,000 members on the site covering more than 200 countries. If you don't get involved, you're missing out.

227. Tour the Organic Farms of the World...For Free

This one requires a little more commitment and although it's easiest to do alone or with another adult, I've heard of entire families going together. Through Worldwide Opportunities on Organic Farms (www.wwoof.net) you can learn and then teach sustainable farming methods in dozens of countries. Wwoofers (participants) are offered free housing and oftentimes free food in exchange for a set amount of work on the farm each day. There are positions in countries ranging from New Zealand to Macedonia and everywhere between.

228. Eco-volunteering

Not all vacations have to be touristy. Eco-volunteering is a relatively new concept that allows you to travel *and* have a positive impact on your destination. Eco-volunteering can include anything from excavating in Jordan to restoring elephant habitats in Thailand. If this speaks to you, follow these steps: 1) Ask yourself, 'What is my passion?' Is it working with animals or teaching English to young

monks in Nepalese monasteries?[43] If you can't think of any, poke around on www.volutourism.org for ideas. 2) Research your options. Contacting potential supervisors directly opens the most opportunities but can be intimidating and shouldn't be tried unless you either speak the language well, have a translator, or they can speak your language. An alternative to blazing your own path is to go through an umbrella organization like those under the volunteer abroad tabs on www.transitionsabroad.com and www.vergemagazine.com. Verge also has links to working abroad and teaching abroad programs.
3) Convince friends to go with you! Here are a few organizations to check out:

- **Earthwatch Institute** - Earthwatch.org offers spaces to work alongside scientists and research teams in 50 different countries. Opportunities include everything from measuring trees across Africa, to tagging sea turtles. Your resume just exploded.

- **Oceanic Society** - Oceanic-society.org. Dolphin studies, ocean conservation, and underwater exploration. Awesome.

---

[43] Two good friends of mine went this route. Free stay, free meals, and dozens of smiling young monks who were eager to learn.

- **Globe Aware** - Globeaware.org is a 'mini Peace Corps' and offers similar opportunities but with shorter timelines.

229. Eco-tourism

This one won't save money, but it deserves mention. While traveling the world is fun, it also has an unpleasant impact on the very environments we're traveling to see. Fuel used to get there and back, items that need to be bought in the new country and then disposed of before leaving, and just the everyday strain of a traveler's lifestyle all have an impact. Eco-tourism is a form of travel in which participants remain mindful of their effects on the beautiful places they visit and make extra efforts to Leave No Trace.[44] Interested in an ecotourism job? Check out the International Ecotourism Society.

230. A Word on Service

Now that we've covered several ways to travel and serve at the same time, we need to take a look at service itself and the unintentional impacts it can have. The desire to help others and the environment is noble and praiseworthy, but you have to make sure

---

[44] Leave No Trace (LNT) is a travel and outdoor ethic aimed to help beautiful places stay beautiful by eliminating the impact of visitors. See www.lnt.org for more details.

what you're doing is for the larger good. There's an old Buddhist saying that goes something like this: "Compassion without wisdom is like having a body but no eyes; your good intentions lead you to do things blindly without seeing their effects. Wisdom without compassion is like having eyes but no body; you can see what needs to be done but won't actually do it. Thus, both wisdom and compassion are necessary." Before setting out to make the world a better place, make sure you understand the long-term ramifications of your actions. I strongly admire those who spend months living with and feeding starving people in impoverished countries, but am sad to see the resulting population booms expand those hungry populations from thousands, to tens of thousands. I've spent time with hungry people and my view isn't based on a lack of compassion, but on the desire for there to be less suffering in the future. This is why we need to make sure our solutions are sustainable and actually have a net positive effect. More people need more food and without outside assistance, the same amount of food that wasn't enough for a few thousand will now be nowhere near enough for ten thousand. This larger population will also have a greater negative impact on the local animal and plant life. I'm not saying we shouldn't help those who need it, we should, but we must be aware of the effects of our actions and decide what to do accordingly.

231. Round-The-World Plane Tickets

On to something more lighthearted. How would you like to have a plane ticket that can be used several times to go to multiple destinations? Round-the-World (RTW) tickets offered by airline alliances do just that. RTW tickets are good for one year and allow you to stop off at multiple locations. You can stay as long as you want in each country, just so long as your total trip time does not exceed one year. If you find a place you love, stay there. When you're through, you can hop on a plane going to the next place. The number of total miles you can travel or stops you can make is determined by the ticket and provider you choose. With a 26,000 mile ticket, for example, all flights can total, but not exceed, 26,000 miles. 34,000 and 39,000 mile tickets are also available. Your other option is to buy a segmented RTW ticket that gives you a set number of flights rather than a set number of miles. With an 8 segment ticket, you have 8 flights to use regardless of their individual length. Tickets usually run $3,000-$10,000 each. Although this is expensive, individual segments often fall around

$300-$400 when you divide it out. You'll get the best deals by starting and ending from countries where prices are lower than in Western Europe or the United States. South Korea, South Africa, Sri Lanka, Indonesia, and Japan are all good choices. Starting from North America is around $2,000-$4,000 more expensive than starting from one of these locations. You can create a mock itinerary on the Star Alliance website or www.oneworld.com. For a more detailed rundown on RTW tickets, see the blog post "How to Buy a Round-the-World Plane Ticket (That Kicks Ass)" on www.fourhourworkweek.com/blog.

232. Live in a College Town

Colleges and universities provide activities, entertainment, and intellectual stimulation. Many movies, lectures, and other activities are free and open to the public. If the finances balance in your favor, take a 1 credit-hour class to get a student ID and access to all the restaurant and shop discounts given to students. Public transportation is even free for students where I live. Ask around to see what other privileges you can get.

233. Become Familiar with Your Local Library (and Support it!)

Everyone loves free things, and your local public library is packed full of them. Mine even has an electronic loan system for eBooks. I can rent books on an eReader or tablet from anywhere in the world, and they automatically return on the return date. While writing this, I'm sitting by a river in Japan and still have access to thousands of books I can actually read (Japanese is too difficult). Call your public library or check their website to see what they have to offer. While we're on the subject, you should frequently ask others what they can offer you. The worst they can say is 'nothing'. Once, when I was in college, I walked into an ROTC office and asked what they could do for me. They didn't know me and I didn't know them, but I knew they had money. So I walked in and asked. The head officer offered me a $1,000 housing scholarship if I took one leadership class, no strings attached. I took the class, shot guns, got the money, and was reassured that the military wasn't for me. This has worked to my advantage multiple times. Visit in person; it's hard to convince people to give you things over phone or email.

234. Self-Educate

And you don't have to do it like you used to. An amazing thing is happening to education due to the influence of the internet. For free, you can take courses and watch lectures online from colleges and universities around the U.S. I'm currently watching lectures from both Harvard and Columbia and don't have to pay a penny. These classes are for educational purposes only, no credit here, but I find it a refreshing change from the 'I'm here to get a degree' attitude so many university students have. 'I'm here to learn' has a much better ring to it. As an added plus, you don't have to do any homework and can go to class whenever you want! Other free sources are wikiversity, an online service combining free learning resources, projects, and research options, and the various free apps for smartphones and tablets that teach everything from foreign languages to photography. We live in a time where we can learn just about anything we want and do it for free. This is an amazing concept. Perhaps the best part is that all these resources and opportunities are on your own time, time you'll have because you don't have to work to pay for them. An extensive listing of free courses, along with free books and other materials, can be found on www.openculture.com.

235. Use Your Friends' Skills and Offer Them Yours

My digital media-savvy friend Taylor designed the cover of this book (thank you!). When my partner and I got married, a wedding DJ friend provided the music, a photographer friend took the photos, a hairstylist friend did hair, and another friend officiated. All professional work and all for free. If you have friends with special knowledge and skills, don't be afraid to ask for their help; you can always offer your special talents in return. Think you don't have any? You do, just brainstorm a bit.

236. Support Your Neighbors and Let Them Support You

Sharing food and labor are obvious ways to do this. Less obvious ones are to split internet and Netflix accounts. This may be illegal.

237. Support Local Stuff

Instead of watching a movie produced on the other side of the country, find local dances or live theatres. These are cheap, more personal, and will leave you with more memories than the movies.

238. Host Community Gatherings

Whether it's a potluck, storytelling night, or a music-playing, marshmallow-roasting bonfire, these events are free and tons of fun. Life doesn't have to be as boring and depressing as many make it; an event every now and then can make a big difference in your feelings of wellbeing.

239. Find Other Options Where You Live

One great thing about local entertainment is its diversity. I live near a well-known storytelling center, miles of hiking trails, and a contra dance hall, as well as tennis, racquetball, and basketball courts.

240. Source Your Hobbies Locally

Use local resources whenever you can. For example, pottery means more (and is much cheaper) when the clay is from your area. If you enjoy calligraphy or Chinese ink painting, collect and freeze Poke berries in late summer – they make a beautiful deep purple ink.

241. Bring Your Own

If you're going to a potluck or party, bring dishes from home. Less trash makes gatherings more enjoyable.

242. Restaurant Leftovers

If you eat out often and anticipate leftovers, bring a food container from home instead of taking that Styrofoam carry-out container.

243. Repurposed Wrapping Paper

Use newspaper or scrap post office packing paper to wrap presents. This is unique, personal, and free. Homemade bows made from strips of nice wrapping paper add a nice contrast. You can even draw your own designs or write messages on the packing paper.

244. Do Your Own Whenever Possible

Whether it's invitations, fruit trays, or decorations, make them yourself. They'll mean more and cost less.

245. Celebrate New Holidays

And do it your own way. I'm a personal fan of Earth Day (big surprise isn't it?) and as it's only a day away from my birthday, we hold a 2-day celebration each year. Look at other cultures' holidays or create your own reason to celebrate.

246. Limit Your Options

Fewer choices frees us from indecisiveness and our natural tendency to second guess decisions. If you go to a restaurant with a five item menu it's easier to find your meal, and be happy with it, than with a menu of 500. This applies to life as a whole.

247. Kill Idle Time

But you're saying, 'Isn't that what we're after?' It isn't. We want to stop working in order to have the time to do what gives us the most joy, to follow what we would do if work wasn't necessary. Although for most of us, our no-work life starts with long days of nothing to do, after a while, whether it be two weeks or two years, idle time turns into boredom. Boredom turns into depression. By all means, spend those first few work-free months lying in a hammock out back doing nothing, but when boredom sets in, it's time to move on to something that gives you a sense of purpose. This is where not having to work really comes in handy; you'll have all the time in the world to pursue your dream vocation and make a substantial change in the world.

By vocation I don't mean job, I mean a calling in a deeper sense. If this calling pays, great; you can work and love what you do. But for many of us, our dream vocation doesn't pay and to pursue it we need freedom of time. I, for example, get great satisfaction helping students from low-income families get into college. I'm not tooting my own horn, I'm just telling you what gives me the most fulfillment regardless of the financial payoff. I want to help these students get access to resources they can then use to improve their own lives. Although this work sometimes pays, most of the time it doesn't. How do you help someone who needs to do well on the SAT but can't afford tutoring? Tutor for free. How can you tutor for free? Make money a non-issue.

That's it. Now you know the basics, and a little more besides, of how to regain freedom of time by living in the middle. There's a lot of life to live, and many new things to discover. We don't have to spend most of our opportunity in 9-5 drudgery. More unconventional (and effective) ways to save, information on building and making the most of the work-free life, and other random useful stuff can be found on our companion site www.livingwellwithoutajob.wordpress.com. We don't update the site often, so be sure to subscribe to get updates as we make them. Good luck with your new life; I hope you enjoy it.

Now there's only one thing left to cover.

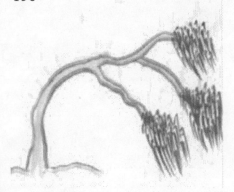

12 Creating Happiness

248. Experience the Small Things

For one meal this week have only bread, cheese, and water. Really taste the food and think of how much effort and how many resources it took to produce it for you. Think of the time it took to grow the grain the bread is made of, and how difficult it would be if you had to make it yourself. Actually taste the water. So often we gulp down our drink eager to satisfy our thirst without really experiencing the in-between. Next time you go outside, stop and listen to the sound of wind-rustled leaves. Appreciate it. If you do this, you can live a fulfilling, happy life without owning much of anything. Happiness is a way of viewing the world, not an item you can acquire. The world has no feelings attached to it and no purpose in and of itself. Analyze reality as unbiasedly as you can and you'll come to realize this. We want life to have a purpose, so we create reasons that it does. Then we call these reasons real. Once you remove these, and it will take time, just as it took time to learn them, you find that the world just exists. Not for any reason, it just 'is'. This is why life can be so great; precisely because it doesn't have an objective purpose. Because of this, you now have the ability to recreate the world in whatever way you see fit, to give life whatever purpose you wish. You can make the world a wonderful place, you already create it each day with the worldview and assumptions you hold. Take charge of that creation.

249. The Most Important Tip

Make yourself happy. Be aware of yourself and your thoughts. Maybe enjoy a cup of tea and 10 minutes of conscious quiet before bed. Wake up early to watch the day wake up with you. When you're happy, you automatically interact with others in a more positive way. This leads to others' happiness, a better society, and better lives for us all. Do it for yourself, do it for your family, for strangers, and for me. So whatever it is, for all of us, ensure your own happiness. This is the whole of this book. Without it, the rest is meaningless.

Made in the USA
Lexington, KY
23 May 2014